Peace
by
Piece

10 Lessons from a Jigsaw Puzzle!

Peace
by
Piece

10 Lessons from a Jigsaw Puzzle!

Laurel McHargue

Nadine Collier

STRACK PRESS

STRACK PRESS LLC | COLORADO

STRACK PRESS

**Peace by Piece:
10 Lessons from a Jigsaw Puzzle!**

Published by Strack Press LLC
Salida, CO

Copyright © 2020 by Laurel McHargue and Nadine Collier
All rights reserved by Laurel McHargue:
laurel@strackpress.com

FIRST EDITION 2020

Library of Congress Control Number: 2020942371
McHargue, Laurel, Author and
Collier, Nadine

ISBN: 978-1-945837-03-6

Cover Design by Sarah Collier
Cover Photograph by Jay Mantri

PRINTED IN THE UNITED STATES OF AMERICA

DEDICATION

To our husbands
—Mike McHargue and John Collier—
who are amazed by and supportive of our work,

and

to all who struggle and puzzle and ultimately succeed!

CONTENTS

ACKNOWLEDGMENTS

Nadine Collier, my forever friend, thank you for sharing your delightfully creative ideas and agreeing to work with me on this book, which never would have been written without you. *We* did it! I look forward to publishing that dream book your Muse recently suggested you should write. Did you hear her say, "Nadine, you should write a book about . . ."?

Mike McHargue, my greatest fan and encouraging husband, thank you for your steadfast support of my work, and thank you for making me laugh after I cry. I never would have completed and published the number of books, podcast episodes, and YouTube *COVID Duck Chronicles* episodes I have out there in the world without your unwavering reassurance and belief that what I'm creating is far better than good. Thank you for saying, "You should keep that colorful puzzle on the table for a while," and for encouraging me to raise ducks. I love you.

Sarah Collier, thank you for this perfect book cover design, and for getting me "back into the saddle" after I completed the monster. I will treasure our friendship puzzle forever.

Linda Ditchkus, thank you for your edits and insightful suggestions. You helped make this book better in wonderful ways.

And sincere thanks to my past generous Patreon supporters for believing in my work: Mary Wilson, Donna Baier Stein, Charlene McDade, Susan and Jim Russo, Jake McHargue, Stephanie R. Sorensen, Joanne Bowman, Erin Sue Grantham, Mary Jelf, Carol Shaughnessy, Judy Cole, and Alex Graham; and to my parents, Pat and Charlie Bernier, who—even from beyond—continue to inspire me. I love and miss you.

INTRODUCTION

From Laurel ~

"You should write a book about . . ."

When I hear these words, and I've heard them often, my brain chuckles and I listen to the idea, which is always offered generously and lovingly. My response is ready:

"I don't think I'll live long enough to write all of the books in *my* head!"

Something was different this time, though.

I had just suffered through and triumphed over a 2,000-piece jigsaw puzzle—the first jigsaw I can remember completing on my own, inspired by a period of quarantine mandated after traveling at the start of the COVID-19 pandemic. I shared my victory with Nadine Collier, my decades-long friend, creative idea generator, and licensed professional counselor (LPC), and she immediately suggested I might write a book about lessons I learned from my experience.

Nadine has completed hundreds of jigsaw puzzles. Pretty sure she could have knocked out mine in a fraction of the time it took me, and possibly with her eyes closed.

I loved the idea.

"Only if you help me, and for real this time," I said. One of her previous suggestions was that I "should write a book about" excuses people make. She would work on a weekly collection and I would add to them, and collaboratively we'd create a new book. I can't remember all the excuses she provided each passing week for why our plan wasn't working (in truth, I had enough excuses of my own), but I should have written them down! As a counselor with a long client list, Nadine didn't need to fabricate reasons for why time had somehow slipped away.

But something was different for her this time too, and together we have created this relatable little narrative. You may discover more than ten lessons in its pages, and that's okay. No extra charge. We spoke with many people during its creation, and their stories embellish our own.

Over the course of weekly Friday morning video visits, Nadine provided resources, ideas, relevant quotations to embellish my narrative, and her own thoughts and questions for reflection at the end of each chapter based on her years of experience as a counselor. Together we created haiku poems to start each new topic. I mulled and dreamed, and as a team, we pieced it all together—like a puzzle.

This time, our collaboration inspired us both . . . and we hope the result will inspire you too!

From Nadine ~

Many have a love-hate relationship with puzzles. I personally love working on them, and they have been a life-saving pastime during many bleak winters in Michigan. I generally begin in November and complete several challenging puzzles by the end of April. This year has been an anomaly, as I've just completed another one and it is mid-July! This 2020 pandemic has really been stressful, and completing puzzles has helped me to pass the time during quarantine in a way that's enjoyable.

Working on puzzles over the years has reminded me of several simple life lessons. I made a list of them to remind myself and to share with my counseling clients. When my dear friend and author, Laurel McHargue, announced to me that she had opened, and was sorting through, the 2,000-piece puzzle she bought during my visit last summer, I was excited for her adventure and just a bit sad that I would not be completing it with her.

But some adventures are meant to be accomplished alone, and I would find, during one of many conversations, that she was learning the same lessons I had. Those conversations sparked the creation of this book.

I hope that you, too, will benefit from these lessons. At the very least, I hope this book inspires you to consider puzzling!

1: PATIENCE AND PERSISTENCE

Patience, persistence
Noble qualities indeed
Remember to breathe!

After removing the clear wrapping from the colorful box, I shook open the lid. Another sealed bag inside the box awaited my scissors. This bag held the treasure—2,000 pieces—and all I had to do was put them together to create a larger, much larger version of the spectacular scene on the box.

How difficult could this be?

The dining room table was prepped, all six feet of its surface completely cleared for the first time ever, awaiting what would come next. I cut open the bag and poured its contents into a heap at one end of the table. And then, after staring at the mess in disbelief, I walked away.

The mere sight of this impossible mound of little squiggly-shaped multicolored pieces was beyond my ability to comprehend. How long would it take me just to turn each piece right side up? Who did I think I was, Houdini? I was no puzzler! The last and only jigsaw puzzle I remembered completing was a little 550-piece fun one, and my friend Nadine Collier had done most of the work.

I walked back to the heap and considered sweeping all the pieces back into the box. No one would be the wiser. I hadn't promised anyone I would take on such a task. As I just mentioned, I was no puzzler. But was I a quitter? It seemed like everyone and their best friends lately were completing jigsaw puzzles, an odd side-effect of this novel coronavirus pandemic. It has affected people in mysterious ways. Puzzling ways, one might say. And I was about to be affected.

I can do this, I told myself, walking back to the daunting pile on the table. *I'll just turn the pieces right side up today.*

And that's all I did for the next hour. It was a small accomplishment, but it felt huge. I smiled.

Everyone knows the way to eat an elephant is "one bite at a time," though I never have and never will eat an elephant. Please don't eat elephants. Or bats. But you get the idea. When a huge task looms over you like a storm cloud, or an elephant, how do you get out from under it?

First, you might have to step back a pace or two and take a deep breath. If the task is something you must accomplish, be it a presentation at work to a judgmental crowd or a personal goal of completing a 2,000-piece puzzle, you must remember to breathe. That's just plain old good advice for every situation life hands you— Breathe!

And you might also consider practicing patience. I like the Cambridge Online Dictionary definition of patience:

> the ability to wait, or to continue doing something despite difficulties, or to suffer without complaining or becoming annoyed.[1]

Waiting. Difficulty. Suffering. Complaining. Annoyance. Just typing those words makes me feel discouraged, and discouragement will stop people from achieving their goals. It's easy to walk away—and stay away—when you become discouraged. It takes *courage* to forge forth into the fray and stay there despite the discomfort.

On day 2 of the great puzzle project, I returned to the table and shook off another wave of discouragement. The pieces, now laid out right side up, took up a full half of the table. And where, oh where to begin?

I was delighted to see that several of the pieces were already linked together, an obvious mistake in the manufacturing process, but my joy was soon squashed by puzzlers online who told me I had to separate the pieces. Otherwise, I'd be cheating. And so, because I wanted to be proud of how I completed this task (another life lesson?), I grudgingly separated the pieces . . . though in truth, I kept them near one another on the table. This little trick—I thought I was so clever!—was pointless, however, because days into the project, I'd rearranged all the pieces in ways too difficult to track.

When you consider the question of where to begin, some will suggest tackling the most difficult, time-consuming part of a project first. Once you finish the hardest part, the rest is easy, they'll say.

I'm not a member of that group. From my perspective, that would be like deciding to link together all the sky-blue puzzle pieces first—which I considered doing until I saw how many nearly identical pieces there were on the table.

Nope. I'm in the group that favors knocking out the easy stuff first, and in the case of completing a jigsaw puzzle, that would be the edge pieces. Get the frame done first. Much like creating an outline for a story plot (not that that's easy, *per se*) or making a checklist of action items for completing a large project, select tasks that are bite-size when compared to the whole.

Now, in the case of my 2,000-piece puzzle, there were 178 edge pieces (I counted them, though now I'm not sure why). Not exactly a quickie task, but at least when I sorted through the chaos on the table, I trusted there'd be a good chance I could easily pick out all of the pieces with one straight edge, or two, in the case of the corner pieces.

I know, I know, there are jigsaw puzzles out there with no borders and no straight edges, but my goal here is not to address *impossible* challenges and people who deliberately like to torture themselves—I'll save those topics for future books.

Although it took several hours to *almost* complete the edge pieces of my puzzle, *almost* completing that task gave me the dopamine rush—that wave of good feeling— necessary to keep me engaged in the project. I had made the decision to continue searching for the next pieces without complaining. I accepted the reality that every phase of this project would require an unknown quantity of time. I evolved from being "not a puzzler" to being someone excited about ultimately completing a daunting project. I would practice patience. Things were coming together, quite literally. And I was hooked.

But why *almost*? I'll get to that in a future chapter. Suffice it to say I was convinced my brand-new puzzle was missing three edge pieces!

Throughout history, people have praised the practice of patience. Take Titus Maccius Plautus (what a great name for a superhero), who lived in a time significantly **B**efore **C**oronavirus. He is credited with saying, "Patience is the best remedy for every trouble."[2] I don't imagine he owned a jigsaw puzzle back in 254-184 B.C., but I'm certain he was faced with challenges far greater.

"What's for dinner, dear?" he'd ask Mrs. Plautus.

"Deer? Did you bring me a deer?" she'd ask. "That'll be ready after he's hung and harvested, salted and dried. There's leftover porridge in the pot. Now, be a love and fill up the water trough so we can bathe this month. Oh, and I'll need more wood for the fire if you want that porridge hot."

It's good to put things into perspective when we become impatient.

A more contemporary source, Shakespeare, expresses the following notion of patience through his character Iago: "How poor are they that have not patience! What wound did ever heal but by degrees?"[3] Sure, Iago is the bad guy in this play, but his words are sensible. And for those wondering about how patience relates to difficult situations between people, these same words apply.

Have you ever been wounded or hurt by another? I have. Ever want to pull out your hair or run away from unpleasant or chaotic situations with others? Oh, yes. Did you take time to breathe before responding? Well, not always.

Some wounds may never heal, I know, and some chaotic situations may seem unbearable (holiday dinners with the in-laws?), but I've noticed if I allow some time to pass, practice patience, and make an effort not to become annoyed—expert guidance Nadine has offered to me more than once throughout our friendship—I've been surprised by the healing that happens, by degrees, while I wait.

Advice is always easy to give, but less easy to receive, and for every word of advice offered, there will be a contradictory suggestion. Welcome to the world of Homo sapiens, though contrary to what our scientific name would imply, we are not all the same. But we all must face daunting challenges every year of our lives, and sometimes every day. Practicing patience helps not only to face those challenges but to overcome them.

When I've overcome past challenges—whether they were physical, emotional, or intellectual—I felt stronger, happier, more self-assured. I learned things about myself. I grew.

My experience with *almost* completing the edge pieces of my puzzle presents me with a perfect segue into the idea of persistence, which reflects elements in common with patience. Again, I like the Cambridge Online Dictionary definition of the word persist:

to continue to exist past the usual time, or to continue to do something in a determined way even when facing difficulties or opposition.[4]

Past the usual time. Difficulty. Opposition. Yuck. Can't we just run away when things become difficult? Well, if it's a jigsaw puzzle, then sure. Sweep the pieces back into the box and donate it to your local thrift shop. If it's a job requirement, probably not. Jobs require persistence for those who wish to remain employed.

I like the idea of doing something in a determined way. Once I made the decision to practice patience, I perceived my puzzle time as a time for quieting the noise in the world. One Zen proverb suggests, "You should sit and meditate for 20 minutes, unless you're too busy, then you should sit and meditate for an hour."[5]

Puzzling became a Zen-like practice for me, and the more I stopped craving the finish line, so to speak, the happier I was with my decision to persist each day, enjoying each tiny accomplishment.

The practice of patience over time naturally translates into an exercise in persistence, and persistence pays off. Lao Tzu asks, "Do you have the patience to wait until your mud settles and the water is clear?"[6] If you don't, you might choke on that first sip. The flavor will certainly be unpleasant. Or if you're wading to the other side, things unseen in your muddy water may trip you up, trap you, bite you. You could drown. You don't want to drown.

Learn how to wait, and the best way to learn is to do. My 89-year-old Aunt Phyllis recently confessed she's still working on being more patient. I suppose her comment might discourage some people, but I look at her continued efforts as inspirational. Despite growing challenges with her vision and hearing, she never complains. She sees them as sources for continuing practice in patience. Clearly, she has mastered the art of persistence by now.

If we're patient and persistent—"past the usual time"—I believe we will discover that mud settles, we will see things more clearly, we will notice the elephant has many parts, we will quiet the chaos in our minds, and we will find the next one-in-two-thousand-piece puzzle link. We might even sleep more peacefully at night.

But where, oh where were those three missing edge pieces? And the bigger question: Could I be satisfied with completing this project if the final result would be flawed?

Nadine's Reflections

How many times in an average day are you required to call upon patience and persistence? If you are like me, it would probably be more than you can count using all your fingers and toes combined. We live in an "I Need It Now" society fueled by constantly advancing technology. Waiting on anything or anyone these days is difficult.

Even though technology aids in making our work and lives easier in many ways, there are still things over which we have no control. This feeling of not being in control is most generally the trigger of our impatience.

The other factor that adds to the equation is unrealistic expectations. If we can learn to accept the things we cannot change and to develop realistic expectations, we will grow in patience and experience dramatically less anxiety and anger.

The act of developing patience asks us to flex our persistence muscle. Persistence requires that we continue to push through adversity, determined to reach a goal.

With these thoughts in mind, reflect on the following questions:

- What types of things test your patience?

- Is your impatience due to a lack of control in a situation, unrealistic expectations, or something else?

- How can you look at the situation differently in order to change how you feel and respond?

- When you are faced with an elephant-size task, how do you handle it? Do you break it down into bite-size pieces? Do you allow yourself to be flexible in your approach?

- Are you patient with yourself and others who may be involved in completing the task? Do you have realistic expectations?

2: TIME MATTERS

Save some for later
Don't fret over what's undone
Live in each moment

With some edge pieces still missing, it seemed that my puzzle project was mocking me. For a third time, I touched every piece remaining on the crowded table—1,819 pieces, but who's counting—certain I'd find those few elusive links. I found myself zoning out occasionally as one unremarkable piece flowed into the next, but I kept at it.

"Aha! Yessss!" I blurted when I found one.

One.

I found only one of the missing edge pieces.

"Just keep going." Cynthia Pemental, a puzzle pro and childhood neighbor from my hometown of Braintree, Massachusetts, routinely posted encouraging messages while I worked on the monster. "They'll turn up," she claimed. Like Nadine, Cynthia has been puzzling for years. She figures she's completed hundreds in her lifetime. She's also the one who told me I couldn't cheat with those pre-linked pieces. I routinely updated her and the rest of the world on my progress by posting photos to social media, and there's a chance I may have quit somewhere along the way if it hadn't been for the enthusiastic encouragement of friends and followers.

Despite Cynthia's belief that linked pieces in a new puzzle pack weren't meant to be gifts to me, I decided that given her experience, she might be right. So, with *most* of the edge pieces linked, I turned my attention to the next task. If only I knew what the next task should be, because—yikes! There were so many pieces in the middle, and from my inexperienced perspective, so many identical ones.

Even though I knew it would be helpful to spend time on another area of the puzzle rather than obsessing over just the frame, which was determined to test my patience, still, it felt wrong to move forward without having successfully completed the first task I set for myself. I'm not exactly a perfectionist, but finding all of the edge pieces should have been an easy task. Time-consuming, yes, but not difficult.

Was Tolstoy's character Kutuzov correct when he told Prince Andrew, "Everything comes in time to him who knows how to wait"?[7] And don't be impressed by this reference to *War and Peace*. I'll read it someday, I promise. I've heard it's a "must read," but like the number of pieces in my ridiculous puzzle project, the number of pages in this classic is daunting. Tolstoy would never get away with publishing a book that beefy today.

But I digress.

If I had insisted on completing the frame before diving into the more difficult sections of the puzzle, I may never have finished it. I certainly would have become discouraged. Rather than succumbing to the notion that I was a failure because I had completed only 98% of the task, however, I gave myself a little slack and decided it might not be the best approach to focus all my attention and all my time on just one aspect of the project.

I would wait, trusting Cynthia and Tolstoy to be correct. Those wayward pieces would ultimately show themselves.

And I would forge forward.

There are those among us, however, who would consider my forward forging unthinkable. We're all wired differently ("Say *what*?"), and there's something to be said for those who will not or cannot quit an unfinished job. There are those who take the notion of persistence to its highest level, and to those rare individuals, I offer my gratitude . . . and condolences. These are the people who get things done, sometimes to their own detriment.

If I were one of those individuals, I'd still be on my umpteenth touching and examining of 1,819 puzzle pieces, and my husband would be on the phone arranging an alternative living arrangement for me.

Back to the idea of what comes next, I'm reminded of a recent podcast episode I narrated in which I shared several mental health wellness tips for quarantine.[8] One of the tips was about focusing on manageable pieces of whatever challenges we face—like the way to eat an elephant (and I'll repeat: Do NOT eat elephants).

Instead of viewing the interior puzzle pieces as one huge chore to tackle, I could identify smaller tasks: blue pieces over here, tiny flowery pieces there, stone walkway pieces here, distinctly structural pieces there . . .

I spent well over an hour rearranging the pieces into smaller sections on the table, all the while hoping those edge pieces would show themselves. And then I selected one of the masses and moved those pieces into the almost-completed frame of the puzzle, where I could work on just that section.

This technique is really nothing new, and when I shared it with one of my West Point roommates, Joanne Cavanaugh Bowman, she told me how she used the idea every day as a single mother of four children—including twins.

"Let's just get everyone through breakfast," she'd tell herself.

"Let me just get them onto the bus."

"Let me just count the children before we head home to make sure I have the same number as I had when we got to the pool."

Joanne's comments reminded me of Eckhart Tolle's book *The Power of Now: A Guide to Spiritual Enlightenment*, which I read shortly after its release in 2004. It impacted me greatly in a positive way, and it's a book I'd recommend to anyone struggling with the notion of time.

"Realize deeply that the present moment is all you have. Make the NOW the primary focus of your life," he suggests.[9] We cannot change the past (yet!), so let go of regrets. We cannot predict the future (accurately), so worrying about it won't be helpful. What you have is right now. Focus on what you're able to accomplish right now.

Joanne compartmentalized every hour of every day, keeping her focus on one discrete task at a time—one moment at a time of focusing just on what needed to be done *now*. And guess what. She never lost any of her four children at the pool!

Nadine and I had a good laugh when we discussed this chapter about time, living in the moment, and saving some "things" for later. The famous marshmallow experiment came up.[10] Left in a room with one marshmallow, children are told they may eat the one marshmallow now, or if they wait a while, they'll be given an additional marshmallow. You might check out some of the hilarious and adorable videos posted online documenting this experiment.

"Pretty sure I'd fail," I said. "That one marshmallow would be gone before the door closed behind the scientist."

"Not me," Nadine said. "I wouldn't touch it unless it was perfectly browned over a fire . . . and until they brought in the rest of the s'more ingredients!"

My husband as a child would have turned up his nose at the marshmallow and requested a meatball instead.

Today, however, I can reframe my marshmallow test failure as a success because if all we can influence is the present moment, then I would have been right to revel in the surety and delectable sweetness of the sugary puff-ball in front of me. There would be no guarantee of a future moment, let alone a future additional treat. No guarantee the scientist would return. And that second marshmallow is never as tasty as the first.

Carpe diem, right?

Let's seize the day, live in the moment, eat that marshmallow, and then return our attention to the next bite-size task we know we can accomplish.

I can't imagine any large project that wouldn't be made easier by using the one-bite-at-a-time technique. The idea of writing a book is daunting, but by applying this piecemeal approach, practicing patience and persistence and focusing on a single "right now" requirement, daunting tasks become doable.

"Let's just come up with chapter ideas."

"Let's just work on the first paragraph of Chapter 1."

"Let's just think about a transition sentence for the next idea."

"And let's eat a marshmallow right now because, you know, energy."

Before we know it, pieces come together and tasks are accomplished. Your child is overwhelmed by a homework assignment? First, let's get it out of the backpack. Let's put it on the table. Let's gather necessary tools (a pencil, a calculator, a dictionary . . . *what's a dictionary*?). Let's look at the first requirement.

Sometimes, the mere act of getting started is the hardest part of completing any major task.

And we can become discouraged quickly. Who hasn't surrendered to negative self-talk at times? I know I have, and it can lead to anger—at ourselves and toward others.

"This is too hard!"

"I'm not smart enough to figure this out."

"Why did they assign this to me? Don't they know I've never done this before?"

And on and on.

Anger and negativity are emotions that deplete our energy. Scientific and scholarly studies and articles abound on the topic of how anger over time can lead to harmful physical manifestations—there's plenty to learn on the interwebs—but it helps to be reminded, also, that time can heal.

In Thomas Mann's *The Magic Mountain* (and no, I haven't read this book either), he writes, "Time cools, time clarifies; no mood can be maintained quite unaltered through the course of hours."[11]

If we allow it, moods, too, shall pass in time. And sure, there are those among us who will cling to negativity and other destructive moods, but they're probably not the ones reading this book right now. They'd likely discount the idea of completing a 2,000-piece puzzle as ludicrous. I almost did. Fortunately, the mood passed. I made the decision to look at each challenging section as a time to focus completely on what I was doing in the *now*.

But even though I had sectioned off different parts of the puzzle's interior, each little scene was a whole puzzle in itself. I found myself overwhelmed—and a little bit bored—by the sameness of all those pieces in that first clump of puzzle parts, and I was tempted once again to call it quits.

Why had I started such a foolish endeavor (negative self-talk)? And where, oh where were those edge pieces (maybe a hint of anger)?

I had to remember I was responsible for deciding how I'd react to my situation, just as we all get to decide how we'll respond to our environment, to the people in our lives, to the challenges put upon us by others or taken on voluntarily.

We get to decide. Isn't that a wonderful thought?

And while it's always easy to focus on the obvious negative qualities in any situation, that makes for a miserable time. I don't know about you, but from my perspective, time becomes more precious each passing year, and I'd rather my days be filled with more positive moments. More peaceful moments.

But, come on. Really. How long would I have to wait, Cynthia and Tolstoy, before those missing pieces would come to me? And what other techniques could I try to overcome my boredom?

Nadine's Reflections

When I was younger, I was rarely concerned with time. In fact, the days seemed to have way more than 24 hours. I would while away the days playing with my siblings. We even turned chores into games. We pretended to be a full-service laundry, we ice danced across the wood floors with the dust mop, and we took the dishes and silverware to the local "pool" in the kitchen.

As I matured, it seemed that time started passing way too quickly. Tasks were no longer fun and games. I learned that "time waits for no one," and took that notion to the extreme. There were deadlines to be met, and consequences if they were not.

Somewhere along the line I forgot how to be flexible, and instead became driven by urgency and the desire to do everything at ultra-high standards. This resulted in many tasks feeling like drudgery and becoming overwhelming. In time I realized I had adopted an unrealistic work ethic and had totally abandoned the creative side of myself that gave me freedom. The worst part of it all was that this ethic had even infiltrated my leisure activities.

When I first started tackling jigsaw puzzles as part of my relaxation time, I found myself setting goals for completion. There were time limits, and I felt guilty if I spent too much time puzzling and frustrated if I didn't complete a puzzle within the desired timeframe. I had forgotten how to live in the *Now*. This realization led me to make changes in my thinking that helped me become more flexible and creative. I got my time back.

With these thoughts in mind, reflect on the following questions:

- What thoughts about time have you adopted?

- How do those thoughts impact your emotions and behaviors?

- What changes can you make to those thoughts in order to allow yourself (and others) more flexibility and help you live in the *Now*?

- What words of encouragement can you give yourself (and others) when struggling with a huge task or problem?

- Have you ever used the "bite-size" approach? If so, how did it help you? If not, are you willing to try it? Why or why not?

3: WALK AWAY!

Walking away when
Difficulty overwhelms
Does not mean failure

Has a person or a situation ever left you feeling exasperated? I can't imagine anyone has led a life completely free of frustrating life events, big and small, and people (big and small) who make you want to pull out your nose hairs and stomp your feet. Although we were never-ever promised a rose garden, when we learned how to avoid the pricking thorns, we could experience the fragrant and stunning beauty of the blossoms.

There were countless blossoms in my 2,000-piece puzzle. I saw no thorns in the colorful patches, but the nearly indistinguishable edges on hundreds of practically identical pieces thwarted my fingertips and accosted my eyes. Every splash of vibrant color taunted me.

"Surely this large patch of pink petals will go together quickly," I told myself, straining over the expansive table to pluck out all the similar colors. I relocated them to the area I believed they belonged inside the *almost* finished edge pieces. And then I stared at them, all those pompous pink pieces, my eyes straining to discern the subtle differences that might help me match at least two pieces.

These two, perhaps.

No? Then, these two.

These two?

No? How about these two?

And then, after several "these two" failures and much like I did after initially emptying the abundant bits onto the table, I walked away. Stomped away, really, with the added satisfaction of murmuring, "Stupid puzzle."

Richard Templar, author of a series of "Rules" books, says:

> Sometimes you have to just walk away. We all hate to fail, hate to give up, hate to give in. We love the challenge of life and want to keep on until whatever we are trying to 'win' has been overcome, vanquished, beaten and won . . . Letting go and walking away means you are exercising control and good decision-making powers—you are making your choice rather than letting the situation control you.[12]

Honestly, the idea of failure crossed my mind. I had already devoted hours of my life to the project—with little to show for my effort—and had decided it would take another pandemic before I'd entertain the idea of starting another puzzle of any size. Did I need to *win* this endeavor? Did I need to show those pieces who was boss?

Yeah. I did. Templar was right. But I could exercise control by walking away throughout the furation of the project whenever I chose to. I meant to write "duration of the project," but I'll use my new portmanteau—furation—which expresses the frequent fury I felt when I considered how long it would take me to complete the puzzle. Fury is too strong a word, of course, for what I experienced—frustration being more accurate—but there were moments of anger.

Instead of staring at that patch of pink and trying to fit every single piece against another, however, I could step back, walk away, make the decision to return to it when I was in a better mood. Like, maybe after that second cup of coffee. Or those five marshmallows remaining in the bag. *And* those five marshmallows.

When something or someone more significant than a puzzle leaves us frazzled, however, it may not be as easy to walk away. But I know firsthand that walking away from people who don't "fit right" can be wonderfully liberating. I'm not suggesting that we run away from everyone who disagrees with us—people who challenge us can help us learn more about the world and ourselves—but there will be those among us whose mission in life is to poke and provoke and pout.

I've never understood "pokes" on Facebook; they elicit a similar response to being poked physically. Ask anyone if they like to be poked. Anyone. Walk away from the pokers. I give my permission to slap away a finger first, preferably before it lands a poke.

And the provokers? The trolls on social media, the instigators of unrest, the spreaders of unkind gossip, why allow them to trouble our lives? Turn away. Don't participate. Stop them mid-sentence and walk away.

Walk away, too, from the incessant pouters. They identify as pouters, they wallow in their poutiness, and they want you to wallow in it with them. Walk away and stay away. We're not going to win them over, and their goal is often to control us and our emotions.

And what if, as you read this, you realize, "Ooo! I've poked . . . I've provoked . . . and I've definitely pouted"? Well, that just means you're human. I'm certainly guilty of all three. Pretty sure I've poked my children to get their attention, and I know they didn't like it. I've been told that at times I come across as being too assertive with my expectations of others, and that has recently cost me a friend. And pouting? Well, life situations are rarely perfect, and we're not like my ducks. Some things stick to our backs and take time to shrug off, but if we don't eventually shrug them off, we can become weighed down, unnecessarily burdened, and persistently pouty.

It can be sad when we realize that we've outgrown a friendship, and it can be a slow process to disengage. Disengaging from relationships that are troublesome or that just don't fit anymore requires work. It requires us to create healthy personal boundaries—those things that define where we *end* and other people *begin*.

As in any relationship, good communication is key to setting clear boundaries. But if we don't speak up and let others know what is acceptable and what is not, the unwanted behavior—like poking—will continue. Unless we want to remain victims to the control others wield over us, we need to find ways to disengage.

We can screen phone calls, return fewer texts, have more important things to do when others want to consume our time. Let's value ourselves and our emotional happiness. Let's say no more often. Let's say "no more."

And then, walk away.

Walk away because we finally value ourselves and our time. Walk away because we don't have to prove anything to anybody. Walk away because enough is enough, because there's more pain and frustration than strength and joy, because this short life deserves to be lived in a better way, because we deserve to live in a better way.

José N. Harris, author of *Mi Vida: A Story of Faith, Hope and Love* says:

> There comes a time in your life, when you walk away from all the drama and people who create it. You surround yourself with people who make you laugh. Forget the bad and focus on the good. Love the people who treat you right, pray for the ones who do not. Life is too short to be anything but happy. Falling down is a part of life, getting back up is living.[13]

And let's remember *we* get to choose what to focus on, who to spend our time with, and how to react to "the bad."

Of course, if what overwhelms us is a job requirement, we may not be able to walk away forever, but we can walk away for a time. A coffee break, at the very least. A long walk. A vacation, if possible, or a sabbatical. And if we still cannot see a solution after we distance ourselves from the requirement, then it might be time to ask for help.

People and events and puzzles may leave us feeling completely unhinged at different times in our lives, and if we're able, it's okay to step away. Sometimes the stepping away is a permanent decision. We might weigh the thorn-to-rose ratio when facing something or someone difficult. Sometimes all it takes is a temporary distancing to work the kink from our neck and the blur from our eyes to see a situation or person or puzzle from a refreshed perspective.

Thomas Campbell agrees. "'Tis distance lends enchantment to the view, and robes the mountain in its azure hue."[14] Living in the Rocky Mountains, I know firsthand how different the mountains appear depending on whether I'm climbing them or gazing at them from my deck. I can't see the summit of a 14er while climbing because I'm too close to it (though it always *seems* too far). While driving away—exhausted, bone-weary, and having suffered some—it's simple to spot.

Sometimes we're too close to people and situations that frustrate us. By stepping away, we give ourselves distance and time to evaluate how we'll respond—to stay away, or to re-engage.

And guess what. Sometimes we may fail to find a solution. The challenge when this occurs is to resist equating failing at a task or a relationship with *being* a failure. Let's not leap to that equation. Let's not allow failures to turn us into that persistently pouty person no one wants to invite for a visit. Let's get up, get dressed, try again, try another, ask for help, and for goodness' sake, stop poking ourselves. Let's be at peace with our tough, uncomfortable decisions, and move forward.

My puzzle predicament was frivolous, but when the idea of trying to find one unique piece was just too overwhelming, when having to hold up the weight of my head while stooped over the hundreds of similar pieces was just too physically painful, I'd walk away knowing I'd return when I was refreshed. And more often than not, when I returned to the table, I would find that one piece easily, almost magically. There were times when I wondered if some force in the universe might be toying with me.

After several days and as many walk-aways—to sing to my fruit trees and water my ducks—I vanquished those pesky pink petals, stood back, and appreciated the beauty of the vibrant, multi-hued tree nestled innocently behind another enormous patch of multicolored flowers.

Ugh. Those flowers were adjacent to the unfinished frame . . .

And then, words from a favorite childhood rhyme made me smile. "Leave them alone, and they'll come home," Little Bo-peep is told, and I walked away finishing the rhyme with a new vision in my head of Bo-peep's sheep dragging those missing puzzle pieces behind them. Such a peaceful little scene.

Nadine's Reflections

It can be difficult to walk away from a situation or person at times. Aren't we supposed to be patient and persistent? Well, yes, to a point. But there comes a time when it may be best to step away for a bit and give yourself time to reflect on the situation or relationship.

It's only human to become emotionally involved in a matter. That's how we are wired. We think, we emote, we behave. Taking time to reflect will enable you to discover the truth about a situation or relationship. It can give you the "break" needed to return to the situation with a renewed focus.

Sometimes we need to set boundaries on ourselves and others in order to maintain our mental and physical health. Boundaries define where we end and another person begins. They determine what we are responsible for and what may be the responsibility of others. Boundaries protect our emotions, our time, our physical health, and even our finances. Healthy boundaries help to form our identity and autonomy. They influence the behaviors of others and are essential to our self-care.

For more information on healthy boundaries, check out the book *Boundaries: When to Say Yes, How to Say No to Take Control of Your Life* by Drs. Henry Cloud and John Townsend.[15]

With these thoughts in mind, reflect on the following questions:

- When have you been so frustrated with a person or situation that you just wanted to walk—or run—away?

- What kind of boundaries can you establish to prevent undesirable behaviors?

- What fears may keep you from setting healthy boundaries? Are those fears realistic?

- What areas of your life are in need of boundaries?

- What would your life look like with healthy boundaries?

- What kind of boundaries have you established in regard to how much time you spend on tasks, activities, and people?

4: THE SUM OF OUR PARTS

"United we stand"
Though we often disagree
"Divided we fall"

Benjamin Franklin is attributed with the following words at the signing of the Declaration of Independence on July 4, 1776: "We must all hang together, or assuredly we shall all hang separately."[16] While this seems a grim message when considering the lessons I learned from a jigsaw puzzle, Franklin's words nevertheless got me thinking about togetherness and what can be accomplished when we're united.

One puzzle piece, different from all the others—even if only subtly—craves connection with another. Sure, I'm personifying these tiny pieces of stamped cardboard, but there were times I swore I could hear their wee voices.

"Hey! Over there! See the one over there in the middle of the pile that looks like me but has three outies and only one innie? That's the one."

"But," I complained, "there are soooooo many pieces with three outies and one innie. It'll take me forever to pick the right one."

"That's okay," the lonely piece would say. "I'll wait. I've got nothing else to do today."

And even though I knew each piece would wait and wait and wait for me to find the next piece that would take me one tiny step forward toward creating a finished product—they have infinite patience, those puzzle pieces—another tiny voice in my head would encourage me to stop whining.

Okay, fine, I'll admit it. I was addicted to the rush I felt whenever I found just the right outies and innies to click together.

"Yessss!" I'd say. Sometimes I'd raise both arms in victory. Sometimes, I'm not ashamed to admit, I'd do a little happy dance.

We're all wonderfully different, but it's inherent in our nature to need one another, not so much to *complete* us, but to enrich us. To make us see that while we're beautiful in our oneness, we're enhanced by our togetherness. Like opposite poles of magnets, we're drawn toward one another for bonds that become difficult to break.

I used to laugh at the old Wendy's commercial with the memorable line, "Parts is parts," and I'm in no way implying that the chicken nugget is anything to applaud (yes, I've eaten my share of them, but only because it was an unstated requirement in those early days of child rearing), but there's something to be said for the notion that the sum is different than—and in many cases greater than—the individual parts.

One puzzle piece. Unless it's the very last piece needed to complete the puzzle . . . or the frame . . . it might appear to be completely insignificant. I mean, what can you do with one puzzle piece?

If you're the creative type, you might come up with several uses. To this day, I cherish a decorative pin my now 27-year-old son made for me from several random puzzle pieces when he was in 1st grade. Pretty sure his teacher had more than a hand in helping to create this memorable Mother's Day gift, but I choose to recognize it as his creation. I get compliments whenever I wear it. But I digress once more.

Certainly, in the case of putting together a puzzle, the sum is greater than the parts, and every puzzle piece counts. And while I appreciate Franklin's sentiment about strength in togetherness, I'm also keenly aware of situations in which the sums of some individuals don't work to create tasty nuggets or peaceful fireside scenes.

People aren't puzzle pieces.

My niece Michelle Russo Stead recently shared a Facebook post from poet and author John Roedel. Roedel presents a fascinating interpretation of people as puzzles, and although he doesn't normally title his pieces, he agreed this one should be called "Becoming." Regardless of your stance on religious affiliation or your belief in a divine being, you might find this exchange enlightening. With the author's permission, I'll share his work:

> Me: Hey God.
>
> God: Hello.
>
> Me: I'm falling apart. Can you put me back together?

God: I would rather not.

Me: Why?

God: Because you aren't a puzzle.

Me: What about all of the pieces
            of my life that are falling down
            onto the ground?

God: Let them stay there for a
            while. They fell off for a reason.
            Take some time and decide if you
            need any of those pieces back.

Me: You don't understand! I'm
            breaking down!

God: No - you don't understand.
            You are breaking through. What
            you are feeling are just growing
            pains. You are shedding the things
            and the people in your life that are
            holding you back. You aren't
            falling apart. You are falling into
            place. Relax. Take some deep
            breaths and allow those things you
            don't need anymore to fall off of
            you. Quit holding onto the pieces
            that don't fit you anymore. Let
            them fall off. Let them go.

Me: Once I start doing that, what
            will be left of me?

God: Only the very best pieces of
            you.

Me: I'm scared of changing.

God: I keep telling you - YOU AREN'T CHANGING!! YOU ARE BECOMING!

Me: Becoming who?

God: Becoming who I created you to be! A person of light and love and charity and hope and courage and joy and mercy and grace and compassion. I made you for more than the shallow pieces you have decided to adorn yourself with that you cling to with such greed and fear. Let those things fall off of you. I love you! Don't change! ... Become! Become! Become who I made you to be. I'm going to keep telling you this until you remember it.

Me: There goes another piece.

God: Yep. Let it be.

Me: So ... I'm not broken?

God: Of course not! - but you are breaking like the dawn. It's a new day. Become!!!

~ John Roedel[17]

You're breaking through, you're becoming, you're not broken. Roedel's dialogue surprised and delighted me, and maybe even made my eyes leak a little. "Quit holding onto the pieces that don't fit you anymore." Why do we find it so difficult to let go—of relationships, of ideas, of socks worn thin? Do these people and things define us? Should we allow them to?

These questions intrigue me. In addition to working on my monster puzzle during days of quarantine and beyond, I also spent many hours sorting through *stuff.* I made long overdue decisions to ditch things I no longer wore or used. I reconsidered longstanding social obligations and even some old relationships. I accepted some loss. And in time, my *letting go* resulted in a greater sense of inner peace.

Things and relationships require care and attention, and it's natural that over the course of a lifetime the quantities of each will increase . . . while the time available to us naturally and inevitably decreases. Rather than letting the realities of passing time depress us, however, I'd suggest we embrace that reality and use it to help us make better decisions about how and with whom we will spend our hours, days, weeks, and years ahead.

I'll be honest. Sometimes *things* aren't so easy to ditch, and I think that's because we create emotional attachments with inanimate objects. Those were my great grandmother's teacups. That was my nana's doily. I've had this spinet piano since I was 10 years old.

When the couple around the corner hoisted my blond Baldwin spinet piano onto their truck, I overcame the pang in my chest by taking a long, deep breath.

"I'm going to play this piano till it just won't play no more!" The man beamed.

I smiled . . . and exhaled.

I hadn't played *my* piano in years. Every day I'd walk by it. Every month or so I'd dust it. Occasionally, I'd run a finger from low A to high C and listen to the reverberation in the hallway. Always, I'd feel guilt over not playing it. Pianos exist to be played. I had to let it go. It was a piece of my life's puzzle that didn't fit anymore.

For obvious reasons, relationships are far harder to let fall away. Yes, I personified that puzzle piece earlier, and I might like to think my piano is happier now with attentive owners, but unless those things are in a Disney movie, I honestly don't believe they have feelings capable of being hurt.

People have feelings, and the hold some people have on others can be stronger than Gorilla Glue. Some holds can choke.

If you're in a healthy long-term relationship, you might already know a few things about how to maintain its health and your happiness. In Kahlil Gibran's *The Prophet,* we're told, "Let there be spaces in your togetherness".[18] Do I love being with my husband? Yes. Do I love hanging out with good friends? Of course. But I'm also a firm believer in quiet time and time to be by myself. The more content we are with ourselves, the more happiness we will bring to our relationships.

Let's respect ourselves enough to carve out uninterrupted time now and then . . . or we may never complete our puzzles.

If we recognize our relationships are no longer healthy, there are things we can do to repair them. Counseling is an accepted and expected step to take. Time apart may provide clarity. Or maybe what's needed is more time together. Sometimes, sadly, two pieces will never fit together well.

In my frustration, I occasionally attempted to force one puzzle piece onto another. This generally happened after hunching over the table for too long or at times when I should have stepped away to do something more productive, like order a beefier pair of tweezers for those pokey chin hairs that sprouted while I was searching for a matching piece.

Sure, I could have forced a couple of pieces, but not without damaging them, and not without distorting the final product.

If force is needed to keep a relationship or friendship together, it might be time to find a way to disengage. But when two pieces come together in a perfect fit—whether the pieces look alike or seem to be completely different— well, that's a beautiful thing. That's a "thing" worth keeping.

When I recall Franklin's words, I'm happy to say I never feared for my life while completing my first 2,000-piece puzzle, though there were times my sore back, stiff neck, and blurry eyes were *killing me*. And yes, I understand the notion of "divided we fall." A puzzle surely is at its best when all pieces are united, but Roedel reminds me that some things fall for a reason.

What reason was there, though, for those missing frame pieces? I really needed to find them, but until I learned—really learned—more lessons, I would have to find peace in knowing they could be gone forever.

Nadine's Reflections

We are all so wonderfully created, with unique gifts and talents. Each of us plays an important role in humanity and together we can do and be so much more! It's really great when we can come together and combine our unique qualities for the common good. We were designed for relationships, and when we connect with those who complement us, it can be a beautiful and enriching experience.

There are times, however, when we can make connections with people or things that drain us emotionally, take more than they give, and cause us to divert our attention from things that are really valuable and important to us. Some relationships and things come into our lives, enrich us for a time, and naturally fall away. Others may cling to us, or us to them, for one reason or another.

We resist purging relationships that are not healthy in hopes that we may be able to salvage some small part that brings us joy. The problem is, you can't just accept a small part of a person. It's a package deal.

Even negative experiences in relationships can enrich your life, though. Looking for the lessons in the experiences will help you make peace and let go of resentment.

In the case of objects we cling to, it's generally a matter of sentiment or cost. We attach emotion or value to an object because it reminds us of someone or of a happy time in life. But, although those objects serve as reminders of someone or something special, the memories and feelings we have are forever stored in our hearts and minds. So, record those memories in a journal, include a picture of the object if you desire, be grateful for the experience, and then consider letting it go.

With these thoughts in mind, reflect on the following questions:

- We all bring special talents and strengths to a relationship. What qualities do you bring to enhance your relationships with others?

- What people or things in life bring you joy?

- Over time, we tend to collect things: objects, titles, friends. Are there things in your life or in your closet that take too much time, energy, space, or money to keep anymore? What are they?

- Are you able to let them "fall away"? If not, what seems to be preventing you from doing so?

- Are you holding on to any resentment? What is it? What will it take to let it go?

- Can you think of a time when you were stronger for having a friend for support?

5: THE LITTLE THINGS

Small things matter most
Or they don't matter at all
We get to decide

Puzzle pieces are little things. Do they matter? Well, yes, to the whole puzzle they matter lots. But does each small piece matter on its own? Nah. Not really.

Depending on whom you listen to, we either should not sweat the small stuff or we should pay close attention to the little things. So, what's a person to do?

The good news is that most choices in life aren't "either/or." It's not "either it matters or it doesn't." Chocolate or vanilla? I'll take a scoop of each, please. Better yet, make that pistachio. And chocolate. Always "and chocolate."

If I'd been eating a little chocolate every day while learning lessons from the 2,000 little things scattered across the table, some of my own smallish things would have become matters of great concern. My decision not to eat while puzzling encouraged me to examine other times when I knew I was allowing unconscious eating to go too far—like right now, as I type these words. Wasn't that bowl of popcorn full just a sentence ago?

Each piece of popcorn is a little thing, but "bet you can't eat just one!" That old *Lay's Potato Chip* ad was right. One handful, maybe, but a handful of salty little crunchy things generally just revs my engine for more. I had to acknowledge my bad habit of always having tasty little somethings within reach while working and puzzling.

Habits are little things. For centuries, people have written about little things and about how small acts can result in something positive. Vincent Van Gogh is credited with saying, "Great things are done by a series of small things brought together,"[19] each of his deliberate brush strokes adding to the next to culminate in a masterpiece; and way before him, Lao Tzu believed, "Great acts are made up of small deeds."[20] If those renowned men valued small things, then who was I not to?

And so, I moved my computer away from the kitchen counter and never brought food to the puzzle table. These were small acts, yes, but they helped me break my bad habit of unconscious consumption. And practically speaking, the tiniest crumb on a puzzle table could wreak havoc. I was having a hard enough time getting some of the pieces I initially had to pull apart—you know, the ones I thought were bonus pieces already joined in the box?— to lay flat on the table.

And don't get me started on crumbs and keyboards. Here's a writing tip for you: don't try to blow crumbs off your keyboard when you still have food in your mouth. Not that I've ever, ever done that, but you know. Just sayin'.

Completing a puzzle project was all about bringing together small things, and with each successful little click of one tiny piece to another, small pictures within the larger began to emerge. When I found the final piece to complete the mast of the ship in the background, I released an exuberant "YES!" and performed a brisk happy dance. I was ecstatic. The boat, one little picture within the puzzle, was finally complete, and with that small success I knew I would have others.

Small accomplishments and small things can bring great pleasure, and as a writer, I feel the joy of finishing one small chapter in a book akin to the joy I felt when I found that final boat piece.

Sometimes I get stuck, though, on what my next word/sentence/transition should be. These are little things when compared to the entirety of a finished book, but they're important.

One helpful technique I've used in my classrooms and in my writing is called brainstorming—a method for breaking through sticking points and generating possible solutions. The idea is to throw forth and write down whatever comes to mind without editing or dismissing any thought. Start with a small thing, like a topic, and let your brain fling out whatever it wants.

Here's how I might come up with ideas for what to include in this chapter about little things:

Topic: ***Little things***—

- Puzzle pieces
- Popcorn pieces
- Ants
- Freckles
- Grapes
- Ducklings
- Babies
- Marshmallows
- Dust motes
- Raindrops on roses and whiskers . . .
- Dimples
- Thimbles
- Subatomic particles
- Words
- Eyelashes
- M&Ms
- Sighs
- Pennies
- Flower petals
- Hummingbirds

My list could go on for pages, but that's the idea. I could write full chapters on each of these little things and whether or not they're important, and that's the beauty of brainstorming. Hummingbirds, for instance, are very small and beautiful things, but they can be intimidating. I'll never live down an initial impression I had about the house we eventually ended up purchasing.

"Militant hummingbirds," I wrote on the paper with the house listing. "Not feeling it."

The previous owners had set up hummingbird feeders—small things—all around the upper deck of the house, and the tiny little tormenters dive bombed us from every angle while we toured the property. Hummingbirds can dive from great heights at terrific speeds, and for such small creatures, they make quite a ruckus. I felt my life was in danger. I knew I could never sit on the deck or enjoy the mountain views without a protective shield. There was no way I was going to purchase a home plagued by hordes of adorable little winged beasts.

Okay, so perhaps I hyperbolized the degree of danger those tiny things presented, but it took some coaxing from my husband before I'd give the home a second look, and now I couldn't be happier. The hummingbirds now get their fill of sugary treats from the trees and flowers on the property and only occasionally buzz us if we're sipping red wine on the deck. They understand the rules have changed.

And now that I've become a duck wrangler, I must admit I've grown quite fond of birds and find pleasure in the different sounds they make. Much like Nadine's husband, John, when I asked him what small things he enjoys, I also enjoy "birdsong on a quiet morning . . . before the gas-powered leaf blowers start up"!

My monster puzzle displayed three birds in flight: an eagle flying to the left and two mallards flying to the right. I decided to search for hints of those little puzzle pieces in the huge blue sky, and while I searched, I was reminded of a book I wanted to reread.

Anne Lamott's *Bird by Bird* is among my favorite memoirs about writing and life. Her book title came from a memory of her father—witnessing Anne's young brother's inability to start an overwhelming school project about birds—telling his son, "Bird by bird, buddy. Just take it bird by bird."[21]

Why is it often difficult to remember to focus on one bird at a time? One bite, one sentence, one junk drawer, one bill, one idea at a time. Just find blue pieces with touches of brown, I told myself, and my birds appeared, slowly, surely, amidst the pieces of sky.

Every day we're faced with small things we need to confront. Every day we need to decide which small things are important and which we can let slide like peas off a full plate. Little things, peas are. My ducklings love peas, so peas are sometimes important.

Some little things are clearly more impactful than peas. As author Sandra Cisneros notes in an interview with AARP, "The older I get, the more I'm conscious of ways very small things can make a change in the world. Tiny little things, but the world is made up of tiny matters, isn't it?"[22]

I'm probably not alone in feeling like there's no way I'm going to make a difference in the world. After all, I'm one small person among billions, one microscopic speck when viewed from space. But Cisneros says small things can change the world, and I want to believe her.

Singer Patti Smith may seem to disagree when she says, "You can't change the world; you can't fix the whole environment." And then she goes on to describe how we can, in fact, do just that. "But you can recycle. You can turn the water off when you're brushing your teeth. You can do small things."[23]

Small things, nascent ideas, tiny acts, all can amount to something greater. A baby becomes an inventor, an idea becomes art, and an act become a movement. These little "things" can change the world, so before I completely discounted my value, I decided I should consider which little things were important to me and which I might fling from my plate.

I generally think most clearly when I'm walking outdoors. There's something in the smell of pine, the mass of mountains, and the crunch of gravel that grounds me. In the course of a brisk three-mile circuit I can solve the world's problems—or at least decide what I'll prepare for dinner.

With an enjoyable break from my puzzle and some focused time pondering all the small things in my life, I returned home renewed, but perplexed. Was completing this puzzle an important little thing?

As tempted as I was to rush back inside and brush the puzzle off the table and back into the box, the completed boat and birds in the blue sky egged me on. How would I feel when I finished the sleeping dog, the walkway, the balcony, the endless sky, the entire puzzle? Would I feel elation? Would I finally know peace?

I'd never know until I found those tiny missing edge pieces, and so, I forged forth once again.

Nadine's Reflections

We often underestimate the impact of the "little things" in life. Some are a distraction, drawing our attention away from more important issues and consuming our time. Others serve to enrich our lives in ways we could never imagine.

How many times have you told yourself that what you do doesn't matter, or that you don't matter? Like a solitary puzzle piece, we question our value and the influence we have in this world. I am reminded of a book called *The Five Love Languages*.[24] In it, Gary Chapman describes how acts of service, quality time, physical touch, words of affirmation, and gifts can have a tremendous impact on our relationships with others.

By learning to speak the love language of another you can grow and enhance your relationship by doing little things. My primary love language is acts of service. When my husband does something as simple as unload the dishwasher while I'm working, without being asked, it speaks volumes to me. I encourage you to give it a try— do something helpful for another person without being asked—and see what a difference the "little things" can make in your relationships, your community, and the world.

Just like a drop of rain on the surface of a pond, your actions and attitudes cause a ripple effect. Take an inventory of your gifts and talents and use them to effect positive change. What you do matters. You matter!

With these thoughts in mind, reflect on the following questions:

- Life is full of "little things." Some are worth our attention, some are not. What little things serve as a distraction, drawing your attention away from more important issues?

- What small change(s) can you make to prevent those distractions?

- Can you recall a time when a "little thing" had a big impact on your life?

- Remember a time you have done a "little thing" that helped someone else, or yourself, in a major way. How did you feel, and what were the results?

6: HELP?

If I ask for help
Does it mean I'm not able?
Does it mean I'm weak?

Okay. I'm just going to say it. I hate group projects—always have. Does that make me a bad person? That I've created this book in close collaboration with Nadine is nothing short of astonishing.

I remember my mother's laugh when she'd tell the story of her first willful attempt at independence, so perhaps my disdain for group work is hereditary.

"I do it myself," she told her mother, who was assisting her with buttons. And did her mother mind that the sweater hung askew when her 3-year-old daughter had completed, proudly, the tricky endeavor? Knowing what I know about my Nana, she probably laughed and hugged her determined child.

When my sons were young, I often did more for them than was necessary, and with perfect justification. It was easier and faster to tie a shoe than to teach the "bunny ears" method, easier to zip a jacket than wait for little fingers to perform the complicated maneuver, easier to do everything for them because, well, I was always in a hurry when they were young and those things had to be accomplished quickly. And how would I be judged if my children's shirts hung catawampus or their laces were loose?

I never considered the notion of personal boundaries or how by overstepping them—however helpful I felt I was being—I might be disadvantaging my boys. Without knowing it, I was telling them they couldn't do whatever task I did for them. I didn't think about what would happen if shoelaces came undone at school and my youngsters might have been too embarrassed to ask for help.

It was, and still is, all about ego. "I do it myself," and I can do it better and faster than anyone else. Ryan Holiday addresses this issue—this bad habit—in his bestseller *Ego is the Enemy* in a section about delegating. When you break up tasks and trust others to complete them appropriately, you build respect and confidence in your team and ultimately, you can complete complex tasks faster. Holiday warns about control, too, and how "it can become paralyzing perfectionism." We might be better off if we learn how to let go of "inconsequential things." [25]

Obviously, the 2,000-piece monster mess on my table could be completed lickety-split if my collaborator, Nadine, were with me to help. I would trust her unconditionally to make short work of the project. After all, the last puzzle I completed and the only one I remember completing was with her. Well, she did most of the work, and I helped find a piece now and then. I could delegate the sidewalk to her, or the endlessly blue sky, or the infinitely intricate patch of flowers.

If she had been around to help me, though, would I have worked through and been reminded of all the little lessons in this book? Would I even have considered writing a book about my experience with the monster? Probably not.

And I also remember that while it was fun to sit with Nadine at the table, I sensed we were competing. Who would get credit for finding that squiggly piece first? Who would find the final piece to complete one of the silly cows in the scene? And when neither of us could find a piece that should have been obvious, my son's girlfriend walked into the room and found it immediately. Our chance for victory was over, the anticipation of being the one to say, "I found it!" stolen from us, the competition between us—which clearly would have determined which of us was stronger, faster, smarter, prettier, more eagle-eyed—ended.

All because of ego.

But . . . but . . . the shoelaces, the zipper, the lasagna—those skills take so much time to master. And sure, I remember that old fishing proverb. We all know it, and I knew it when I was a young mother, but I still chose the easier way too often. "Give a man a fish and you feed him for a day; teach a man to fish and you feed him for a lifetime." But . . . but . . .

Many hands may make light the work in my kitchen, but if I ask for help, or if help is offered, in addition to spending more time pointing out where the spices are and which ones are needed, aren't I placing a burden on another person? Maybe they're offering out of politeness. Maybe they really just want to sip wine while I buzz around my kitchen effortlessly whipping the ricotta with the egg and parsley, par-boiling the noodles while caramelizing the onions. Maybe if I accept the help, they'll add something I hadn't considered to my recipe.

And maybe I might learn something from them. Maybe my lasagna will taste even better. Would that even be possible?

Asking for help can be a good thing, particularly as we mature. I believe it's necessary to keep learning and challenging myself as I age so I don't fall into routine ruts and become boring. As I age, though, my entrenched ego might interfere with my better judgment. I might refuse to change my lasagna recipe because it's always been delicious and earned me adulation in the past.

I might put words and thoughts into other people's mouths and minds. I might decide my friend would rather sip wine than stir my sauce when in truth, she would feel rewarded and appreciated if I accepted her offer. I needed to remind myself that by asking for help, just as by helping others, both parties can benefit.

But what if I don't feel I *need* help? It's not like I'm unable to make the lasagna by myself, but by accepting a friend's offer of help, I'm making my friend feel valued—and as a bonus, giving myself more time to enjoy some Pinot! It's a win-wine!

At times when we feel we don't need help, we might be in the perfect situation to bolster another person by accepting their offer of help.

Another thing I've noticed as I've matured is that challenges often become more, well, challenging. Have I mentioned the blurred vision, the stiff neck, the sore lower back from hours of hovering over my puzzle? And why didn't I tackle a monster puzzle when I was a few decades younger?

Oh, right. A few decades ago, coronavirus wasn't a life-changing, time-changing phenomenon. I was actively engaged in jobs and child-rearing and socializing.

It's funny how I've considered doing things I never would have considered before the planet was put into lock-down. In addition to working on the puzzle, my decision to raise ducks from day-old hatchlings delivered through the United States Postal Service mandated putting their needs before my own to keep them alive and thriving. I had to take puzzle breaks to care for them and laugh at their adorable antics. They couldn't ask for help, but I knew they needed it, and it made me feel good when I heard their happy peeps of thanks. More small things.

Saying the global pandemic has been difficult would be an understatement. It has impacted people in ways yet undefined, particularly in terms of isolation and its long-term effects. Not everyone is able to experience as I have the mental health benefits of duck wrangling. Most of us thrive when we're among others of our species, and quarantine requirements have put the kibosh on most social gatherings.

Truth is, we need one another. My five little quackers stick together in everything they do, clearly finding comfort in their togetherness. They eat together, swim together, preen together, run around the yard together, and fall asleep in one delightful feathery heap. Their togetherness helps them learn and ultimately survive. But they're just birds.

People need the help of one another too, and I'm not just talking about when we can't open a pickle jar or worse, remove the "easy off" safety seal on the mayonnaise. I'm talking about helping one another with the important things—the debts, the disappointments, the misunderstandings, the deaths—and sure, sometimes the cooking. I've been listening to lots of *oldies* lately, and in Bill Withers' song "Lean on Me," he mentions pride.

"Swallow your pride," he says.[26] Maybe that's why I still have trouble asking for help. Pride. Ego. I can do it on my own. But Withers presents an offer of help recognizing that in his humanity, he may soon need help himself. It's human nature to need help every now and then, and I believe it's in most people's nature to want to help others who are struggling.

As in Withers' song, lyrics from The Beatles' iconic song "Help" also lament the inevitable difficulties associated with growing older,[27] though they don't mention pickle jars. Sometimes we must ask for help, and that can be a humbling experience.

I appreciate this quote about humility misattributed to C. S. Lewis: "Humility is not thinking less of yourself, it's thinking of yourself less."[28] I love these words because they don't diminish us. We don't have to feel *less than* if we find ourselves in need of help.

As a former Army Officer, I've been on both ends of the "needing help" equation, and the concept of selfless service—of considering the needs of others and of the team before your own needs—is ingrained in all who serve. It's expected.

It doesn't require military service, however, to recognize that regardless of the type of team we belong to, members who act selflessly will be infinitely more valuable to the group than those who seek personal gain.

When we find our place in a group, when we offer and are willing to accept help, we can positively impact our world, even in small ways. Just as individual puzzle pieces are significant in relation to the entire completed scene, each one of us—when joined with others—has a purpose, a place, a significance.

Being humble doesn't mean we aren't significant. Each of us has a purpose and a place in this world, and we needn't boast that we're any better than anyone else. We need others to complete the picture, the task, the mission, and to recognize our own significance.

That said, we don't *always* have to ask for help. Personal struggles and challenges aren't always bad things. It's often important to tackle tasks independently. At some point, young ones deserve to experience the joy of snuggly tying their own shoes, correctly aligning their buttons, and cooking a pasta dish worthy of praise.

And when it came to my jigsaw monster, although I'd have to forego the companionship, the laughter, the faster completion, and the shared victory beverage, I wanted to experience the challenge of completing a 2,000-piece puzzle alone.

I wanted to find all of the squiggly pieces by myself, wanted to lift that last piece, if ever I could find it, to my lips for a victorious kiss—a ritual Nadine shared with me—before clicking it into place and doing the happy dance. I wanted to "do it myself," to experience the feelings of peacefulness and joy that come from a difficult job completed, if only to prove that I could.

So, even if ego is the enemy sometimes, I'll argue there's also value in completing a project independently. If my mother were here, she'd agree. And she'd likely find those missing frame pieces lickety-split.

Nadine's Reflections

Why is it so hard for us to ask for help? Does pride get in the way? From a young age we strive to achieve independence. It's good to challenge ourselves. That's how we learn, grow, and become. I have no trouble asking people to help when I am working on a task that I consider a team responsibility. But, there are many other times when I resist asking.

My reasons? I don't want to inconvenience anyone, I don't want to look weak, I want to be in control of the situation . . . the list could go on and on. There are a variety of reasons we can give for not requesting help, but are they driven by healthy attitudes or negative ones?

If your goal is personal growth, it is understandable that you would desire to complete a task on your own. But it is possible to experience personal growth as part of a team effort as well. Interpersonal skills can always be further developed and there is no better way than by working with others.

A team effort also gives the opportunity for others to grow and flourish when you ask for and allow their help.

With these thoughts in mind, reflect on the following questions:

- Do you consider yourself a team player, or are you an "I'll do it myself" person?

- Remember a time when you completed a project on your own. How did you feel? Was it difficult?

- Have you had that *competitive* feeling when working on a project with others? Do you see that as a benefit or detriment to successful completion of the project?

- Are you able to ask for help? If not, what prevents you from doing so?

- Is there a task confronting you right now that would be more easily or safely completed if you had help? If so, will you ask for—and allow—another person to help?

7: FOCUS

Presently focus
Yesterday and tomorrow
Don't exist right now

Yesterday I recorded a new podcast episode about how my feathered friends are helping me survive the pandemic and why I cried last week. It is done, aired, and behind me. Could I change it? Eh. I suppose I could delete it, but that's not a thing I do. Things done are done.

Every day I could worry about how people might respond to what I create, but I've learned from years of publishing books and short stories that how people respond is something over which I have no control. Once my work is "out there," it belongs to the public and is open to each consumer's interpretation. As a creator, I must be okay with that. And unless I've created/said/done something purposefully and personally offensive, it's not helpful to expend my energy fretting.

There are those who choose to live in the past, and what I've noticed about those people is their focus on regret and how that regret leads to feelings of depression. I'm all for trips down memory lane now and then. I'll pull out the photo albums (such relics!) and listen to oldies music, sometimes even allowing a memory to leak from my eyes, but when the music stops, I'm always happy to be where I am today.

Tomorrow I'll be working on a new short story for a contest, but I don't have the prompt yet. I'm excited to see what genre they'll assign me, but I can't start writing it until that happens. If I were to stay focused on the future, I'd become anxious. What if I get a genre I'm not comfortable with? What if my Muse abandons me? What if I lose internet connection and can't upload my submission in time? And who knows? Tomorrow is hours and hours away, and I may be abducted by aliens tonight, so why waste energy puzzling over the assignment?

Ooo! Maybe they'll assign a science fiction prompt! I could write about—

No, Laurel, focus! Focus on what you're doing right now. Focus on writing this chapter about focus. See how easy it is to lose focus?

My husband (perhaps too frequently) will shout, "Squirrel!" And when he does, I know my attention has wandered from whatever task has lost me. I'm not a pro at focusing on each moment of each day, but I know I'd be far more productive if I could improve on that skill, and I do try to remember this.

The Buddha was a pro. He is credited with saying, "Do not dwell in the past, do not dream of the future, concentrate the mind on the present moment."[29] I sometimes wonder what it would be like to live in a monastery, in a place isolated from the modern world, in a place without clutter or cell phones or the Internet, in an attitude of constant mindfulness, without judgment, without the expectation I should be a brilliant multitasker. But if I never dreamed of the future, if I lived only for right now, would I set any goals for myself? And did squirrels exist in Ancient India?

I don't totally buy into the "no future dreams" philosophy. I agree that dwelling in the past is counterproductive, and I understand the benefits of being present in each moment, so two out of three ain't bad. Right, Buddha?

Have you ever been in a conversation with someone and you notice their eyes wandering to another person, to something behind you, to a dog chasing a squirrel? I have, and I recognize the person is not with me. They're somewhere else. And it has made me feel disrespected, unworthy, unimportant.

It takes practice to be *with* someone when we're with them, to forget about what we should cook for dinner and the mean thing someone said about us yesterday. We live in a world of multitaskers, of bullet-point summaries and shorter, more frequent commercial breaks, and our brains are adjusting to fast-fast-fast.

I moved my computer to a quiet corner in my bedroom because when I worked in the kitchen, there were squirrels everywhere. A dirty cup I should put into the dishwasher. Peanuts and popcorn on the counter within easy reach. Crumbs on the counter to be swept into the compost bin. A compost bin I should bring to the garden. Weeds in the garden I should pluck and bring to my ducks. Mud on my garden shoes from plucking for ducks. A kiddie pool needing fresh water, and I might as well water the trees while I'm at it.

And the monster puzzle downstairs calling to me like a siren song, though not as dangerous.

You get the idea. "Squirrel!"

Completing a 2,000-piece puzzle, like completing any hefty project, requires concentration and purposeful focus. There was no way I could finish this project quickly, so I had to accept the slower pace. I had to make the decision to block out the extraneous tasks and to be present and mindful each time I approached the table.

One definition of mindfulness from a Google dictionary search (because who—besides Scrabble nerds, Nadine—owns a print dictionary anymore?) is:

> a mental state achieved by focusing one's awareness on the present moment, while calmly acknowledging and accepting one's feelings, thoughts, and bodily sensations, used as a therapeutic technique.[30]

When I think about monks, I think about how peaceful they are, and despite their ascetic lifestyles, how happy they seem to be. Their lifestyles appear to be therapeutic.

When I was able to focus, really focus on my puzzle, I understood the therapy of being mindful. Modern day Vietnamese monk Thích Nhất Hạnh is credited with saying, "The feeling that any task is a nuisance will soon disappear if it is done in mindfulness."[31]

There were many times when I felt the weight of all those pesky pieces was simply too heavy, too burdensome, too much of a nuisance. But when I approached my puzzle table willing to find just one connection, the negative feelings disappeared, and my focus sharpened. Rather than having my eyes glaze over, I could see the tiny details—an itty-bitty sliver of color on the edge of one piece, a hint of something that could be part of a reflection on the water.

During those times of purposeful focus, I always found far more than one connection. I would notice the oh-so-subtle difference in hue between two blue pieces of sky. A piece with a wispy squiggle fading to violet would practically transport itself to its appropriate squiggly space within the frame. I really like those squiggly pieces. And I would notice myself smiling contentedly.

That degree of intense and purposeful focus was therapeutic. I experienced enjoyment, pleasure, and happiness in those moments, and not only because each new click brought me closer to finishing the project. I let everything else go—the cups, the crumbs, the weeds, the ducks—and chose to find fulfillment in being completely present in the tiny task of finding one matching piece.

My friend Hillery McCalister reminded me recently that the process of putting together a puzzle is more important than the result. She inherited her mother's hefty collection of 1960s puzzles with pieces missing and edges chewed on by the family dog. Hillery is a singer-songwriter, among other wonderful things, and she likens the way to approach a puzzle to the way she creates a song, with an open mind willing to engage in some mental gymnastics, and as a meditative activity.

Some puzzlers will complete a puzzle once and pass it on, never to imagine redoing it at some future point. I was fairly convinced I'd never want to see my monster again, if or when I ever completed it—until Hillery told me about her mother's practice.

Her mom would recreate the same puzzles again and again, enjoying the nostalgia of returning to an "old friend" or favorite scene and facing it in a fresh way each time. She wouldn't always complete the frame first, a fact which encouraged me to forge forth despite my own missing edge pieces. And she would challenge herself, recording the time it took her to complete a puzzle on the inside of the lid, attempting to best her last time.

Hillery's solution to the missing pieces in her puzzle collection? She would draw them onto pieces of paper! What a creative solution to a problem that could stop some people from even starting a project.

Missing a piece of a project? Improvise. Stretch your brain in new ways. Accept the flaws with a smile and a willingness to make the most of your moments along the way. Thích Nhất Hạnh reminds us that "the present moment is the only time over which we have dominion,"[32] so recognize that it's up to us to decide how we'll face each new challenge and each new moment.

American psychologist Tara Brach asks, "What would it be like if I could accept life–accept this moment–exactly as it is?"[33] And so I always do my best to look into the eyes of people I'm with, to listen to what they're saying without judgment and without finishing their sentences for them, without formulating my response before they finish, without searching for something more interesting to see or say. It's not always easy.

And I learned to accept that even if I didn't match a single piece with another during my daily session with the monster, I'd value the therapeutic, meditative, peaceful qualities of my focused time.

It takes mindfulness. It takes practice. It takes a desire and a decision to value those I'm with and whatever I'm doing.

If I had remained focused on finding those missing frame pieces when I started puzzling, I would have stayed stuck in the past. I would have floundered in my frustration. I might never have moved forward. I might never have—spoiler alert!—finished the puzzle.

But I didn't stay there. I believed my neighbor Cynthia when she promised they'd show up, and I refocused my search on center pieces.

Mindfulness is a decision I get to make every day, and unless I purposefully make the decision to be fully present in whatever I'm doing, it won't happen. If I don't choose to be mindful and focused, I allow the squirrels to dominate my day.

Believe me when I say there's nothing peaceful about unfettered squirrels—there's a ridiculous story about that for another book. Personal experience has shown me how squirrels can rule and ruin a day.

They might even sneak into your home and run away with puzzle pieces.

Nadine's Reflections

There are times when focus is required while working on a jigsaw puzzle. With so many shapes and colors to sort through to find just the right piece, our determination can cause us to get "stuck" and unable to move forward. At other times our focus can easily be distracted, and we give up to start on something else.

The same thing happens in many life situations. You may find yourself stuck dwelling on something that happened in the past. You cannot go back and change what happened, and living with regret will only lead to depression. On the other hand, you could be distracted by thoughts of what may happen in the future.

Focusing and fretting about things over which you have no control will lead to anxiety. Your best option is to keep your focus on the present moment. One helpful way to do that is by practicing mindfulness. The goals are to learn how to be content in the present moment and to acknowledge all aspects of the situation you are currently experiencing, including your own emotions and bodily sensations.

With these thoughts in mind, reflect on the following questions:

- Do you find yourself focusing too much on the past? Is there a particular incident in the past that seems to preoccupy your thoughts?

- What types of things in the future do you tend to fret about?

- Becoming mindful is a practice that will enable you to enjoy the present moment more fully. You may want to take time to meditate daily. Mindfulness doesn't just happen; it is a conscious choice. Take a few minutes right now to soak in your surroundings. Use all your senses: What do you smell? Is it pleasant or unpleasant? What colors and shapes do you see? What textures do you feel? What is the temperature of the air? When you taste something, take time to consider how it feels in your mouth. What taste buds does it awaken?

- Are there "squirrels" ruling your day? How do you get yourself back on track?

- What can you do to prevent those "squirrel" moments and remain focused on the present task?

8: A DIFFERENT PERSPECTIVE

Is the glass half full,
Half empty, or twice as large
As it needs to be?

(George Carlin is credited with saying this, though
not in haiku form!)[34]

Nadine and I have shared a conundrum I believe most
puzzlers have faced, and frequently. We stare at the many
pieces before us, studying the shapes to find the one that
will fit an empty space perfectly. We see it—seemingly
the same shape and color that is missing—only to find it
doesn't fit. We try it again in disbelief, sometimes
applying just a bit of extra pressure. Surely it will fit if we
jiggle it just a tad. But no. It's definitely not the piece we
expected it to be.

How could our perceptions be so *off*?

"We don't see things as they are, we see them as we are," said Anaïs Nin, a 20th Century diarist.[35] I know if I'm impatient or if I already have my mind made up about something, I'll make mistakes, I'll misjudge a situation, I'll see what I expect and want to see. If I'm feeling unsure of myself, I might even put thoughts and words into other people's minds and mouths, and as Shakespeare's King Lear recognizes, "that way madness lies."[36]

When I was four months pregnant with our first son, I asked my husband if he was excited about the upcoming birth, and his response was less than enthusiastic. It didn't take much for my fitful tears to flow along with my interpretation that he didn't want our unborn child.

"But you don't even *look* pregnant," he cajoled, trying to comfort me. "He's not even here yet. I'll be excited when he's born!"

He then offered to stand on his head if it would make me stop crying . . . and I forgave him immediately for responding to my pregnancy-rattled question in a way I neither wanted nor expected.

Nadine recalled a tiff with her husband over something small. They had just finished some yard work and were putting away the various tools they'd used, one of them being a large tarp. Nadine had carefully laid it out flat, waiting for her husband to take one end so they could fold it. In her mind she had concocted the ideal (right) way to fold it. When her husband picked up his end of the tarp, she started to direct the process, but he had another idea, having done this several times before. She became frustrated—almost angry—that he would suggest another (better) way.

After ceding to him in the battle of the tarp, she wondered why she had gotten so emotional over something so insignificant until it occurred to her that she had taken his suggestion as a personal insult to her intelligence. She thought he was telling her that her way was stupid—that *she* was stupid—though he had never said those words to her in all their years together.

In her role as a counselor now, she recognizes what she (and I) experienced then was *cognitive distortion*. When you experience a negative emotion—anxiety, depression, anger—it's a signal that you're possibly misinterpreting the situation you're facing. And if you can identify the emotion and accompanying thoughts, you can then discover a possible distortion and find positive alternatives that may be true or truer than what you originally perceived.

My husband couldn't experience the emotional upheavals I suffered, and Nadine's was simply completing a task he'd performed efficiently countless times before. There was no malice, no judgment from them. We were the ones fabricating those negative interpretations.

When I searched "cognitive distortions" on the Internet, out of the 15 common ones listed,[37] I was embarrassed by how many of them I recognized as having influenced me over my lifetime.

"Jumping to conclusions"—But honestly, doesn't everyone do that?

"Personalizing"—Who, me?

"Always being right"—Well, I'm always right *sometimes*, aren't I?

I could go on, but then I know you'd judge me harshly, and you'll make me feel really, really bad about myself ("Blaming").

Go ahead and check out some of the other ones and see if maybe, just maybe, you may be falling victim to distortions in your thinking. And then, don't despair. Nadine recommends a book called *Feeling Good* by Dr. David Burns in which he outlines techniques for recognizing and straightening out those falsehoods.[38] Maybe I should read it.

Oh, right, I shouldn't *should* on myself.

It took a few wrongfully forced pieces while working on my puzzle to understand that many seemingly "right" pieces would never fit where I wanted them to fit, so I needed to look at the pieces from a different perspective. I needed to recognize—as my Aunt Phyllis reminded me in a recent conversation—that round pegs won't fit into square holes. Well, unless the round peg is smaller than the square, and then it would fit . . . but there would be open spaces in all the corners, and I just know it would feel as out of place as it would look.

I should (oops!) stop personifying inanimate objects.

Perhaps if I approached my puzzle from the other side of the table, I'd find the right pieces for the appropriate spaces.

I'll credit my 5th grade teacher with encouraging me to see things from a different perspective, though I still have to remind myself to do just that. My youthful class enjoyed frequent "field trips"—to the field next to the playground. Ms. Woods would have us prone in the overgrown grass so we could peer through the chaos and imagine what life would be like living as a tiny creature among the blades. She'd have us flip onto our backs and lose ourselves in the slow-moving, dizzying cumulus clouds.

"Now, write a poem about what you see and how you feel!"

She was a hippie. She made us feel larger than life and tiny as a spec, but always she made us feel significant.

I copied her field trip technique when I taught 7th grade Language Arts, and after brushing off the grass and returning to the classroom, I asked students to stand on their chairs or desks to see their surroundings from a different perspective. Not all complied. Some looked at me as if I'd just sprouted an extra head.

It wasn't as powerful as the "O Captain! My Captain!" scene in the film *Dead Poets Society*,[39] but it was an exercise in having students do what they'd never been asked to do before, and I was happy one bold boy didn't electrocute himself when he reached into an overhead light.

There was laughter. There was a palpable sense of excitement. The experience may even have changed a few minds about how those young students perceived teachers.

Art teachers will often encourage students to position paintings and drawings upside down when tasking them to re-create an image because it forces them to observe lines and shapes from a fresh perspective. The curve of an eyebrow, the ripples on a lake, the angle of a rooftop all appear different from an upside down perspective, and the budding artist must draw what they see, rather than what they expect to see in a familiar object. Results from this method are surprisingly more accurate than if the student had attempted to copy the artwork right side up.

In past years I've reframed several special paintings I inherited from my parents, and each new mat and frame transformed the art within. I was always delighted with the result because it changed my experience with the artwork. I'd notice a fleck of color I'd never seen before. I'd learn something new about the art.

Much like reframing a painting, if we purposefully reframe personal interactions by considering them from a different perspective (maybe from another person's perspective?)—by stopping ourselves when we want to fill in the next sentence or interpret an expression based on past experiences and on what we expect—we just might learn something surprising about what the curve of that eyebrow really means.

It's all about perspective, and the good news is if we learn how to be mindful of our emotions and to identify times when we might be overreacting or misinterpreting, we can take a step back, look at the situation from a different angle, and make a better choice about how we're going to respond.

Whatever we do, beware of "making a mountain out of a molehill." Who hasn't heard that more than once in a lifetime?

I now recognize my mother would occasionally do just that, one of the 15 common cognitive distortions: catastrophizing. Don't tell her about your hangnail or she'll anticipate gangrene followed by amputation. Maybe all mothers tend toward extremes when it comes to their children's safety. Not me, of course. My children were never injured because remember? I did everything for them.

"JK," as the young'uns today would say, but all kidding aside, I recognize how my perspective has changed on many things as I've matured, and in mostly positive ways.

So when I started to feel like a failure, like there was no way I'd ever finish that stupid puzzle or find those missing pieces, like I was just going to prove to myself I couldn't finish this thing I'd started, well—I reminded myself to step away, to do a little dance, and to stand on a chair at the far side of the table for a fresh perspective. I might even have muttered, "Get a grip! It's just a puzzle!"

And then I walked away, poured myself a glass—just the right size—of a tasty beverage, and remembered to breathe.

Breathe.

Ahhhhh.

Find a peaceful place in your home and in your heart and breathe.

Nadine's Reflections

Your perspective can greatly impact your interpretation of a situation. Some people take a generally negative view of life, where others are more positive or hopeful. Two people can have exactly the same experience, yet interpret it differently. You may be wondering how that could be.

Well, Cognitive Behavioral Therapy (CBT) posits that our thoughts dictate our emotions and behaviors. If our thoughts are negative, we will experience negative emotions and behave in unhealthy ways. Think of your brain as a very high-tech filing system. From birth, you have been filing away things you have learned from various experiences, people, and media. Each new experience you encounter is filtered through that information web.

Over time, with reinforcement from certain experiences, you develop a "script" of thoughts. That script can tend to include some thoughts that are distorted and may influence how you react to situations you encounter. When you find yourself becoming over-anxious, depressed, angry, frustrated, etcetera, it's good to take a moment to check your thought script and challenge it. You may find other, more appropriate thoughts that will reduce your negative emotions and help you respond in a better way.

You can read more about "stinking thinking" and how to change your "script" in the book *Feeling Good* by Dr. David Burns. If you are having a persistent struggle with negative thoughts, you may want to consider seeking counseling, either in person or on an online platform.

With these thoughts in mind, reflect on the following questions:

- Do you generally see the glass as *half full* or *half empty*?

- Who do you talk to, or what do you do, to help you gain a different perspective on a situation?

- Remember a recent incident in which negative thoughts or distortions caused your perspective to be out of focus. How did you feel and what were your thoughts?

- Take a moment to challenge those thoughts. Are they absolutely true? What evidence supports your thoughts? Are there other, more positive thoughts that are true or truer?

9: LOOK BELOW THE SURFACE

Below the surface
Mystery, chaos, beauty
And puzzle pieces

After rereading Shel Silverstein's *The Missing Piece*[40] to see if I might find a clue (I didn't) and making peace with the fact I might end up with a 1,998-piece puzzle, my husband asked, "Have you looked under the table?" I could tell he was getting bored by my daily discourse on the missing pieces and how I'd have to write to the puzzle manufacturer about my disappointment.

"Of course I have. I've looked all around the table. Twice."

I hadn't actually looked *under* the table, because how could pieces end up there? I'd occasionally brush a piece off the table while leaning over the puzzle. That happened many times during my three-week effort. Pieces might land on a chair or bounce off my knee, but I'd find them easily on the floor directly around the table edge.

"But have you looked *under* the table?" Mike persisted, and I resisted falling into the cognitive distortion trap of accusing him of accusing me of being stupid. My inclination to go there was surprisingly swift, though. It's amazing how easy it is to perceive a helpful comment as an accusation.

And so, after one more journey around the edges—it's a large table—I pulled out the chairs and got down on my knees.

Well, butter my bread and call me silly. Lo and behold, under the very center of the table, upside down and nearly the identical color as the carpet, lay my missing pieces. Suddenly, the day appeared brighter and all was right in my world. As a bonus, though I needed no bonus, Mike never said, "I told you so."

I performed a longer than usual happy dance.

There remained more than a quarter of the pieces still unattached, about 500ish, but after clicking together those missing edge pieces and finally finishing the frame—such satisfaction!—I was energized to push to the finale. I could stop obsessing over how strongly I'd word my letter to the jigsaw puzzle factory. I could finally sleep through the night. My puzzle was becoming a thing of beauty.

Things of beauty. We've all heard the expressions about beauty being only skin deep and how we shouldn't judge books by their covers. Those are mere surface things. The wrapping on a package hides its contents and can deceive.

It's important to look below surfaces, and not just for puzzle pieces. I learned long ago never to buy a shiny used car without checking under the hood. Why? Because the engine could be rusted, wonky, missing. Don't buy a house without checking the wiring, the plumbing, the skeletons in the closets. Why? Same reasons. No one wants a wonky skeleton. And don't marry someone until discovering how their mind works. Could be all kinds of surprises going on in there.

Wow, Laurel. You got all of that from your jigsaw puzzle?

No, of course not. But working on the monster reminded me of many things I'd been taught and learned over the years. See, I am now "of an age" where in addition to losing puzzle pieces, I also occasionally cannot find those vitamin D supplements that roll off the counter and disappear on the hardwood floor. Why is it always the translucent pills that roll away? This is to say I have several decades of learning under my well-worn belt.

And despite my decades, I'm grateful I still can get onto my knees, crawl around with my spectacles on, find missing pieces, and stand back up again . . . and that I haven't yet lost my marbles, though some of you reading this right now might raise an eyebrow.

I've also learned the most destructive part of an iceberg hides beneath the surface of the water, and calm countenances can mask inner turmoil.

When I decided to join the Army, my father advised me to "play the game" in order to succeed. He warned me not to cry in the presence of those who'd try to make me cry, and never to volunteer. Keep a low profile. Wear a (figurative) mask.

His advice was sound, and over the years I discovered people often wear different masks in different situations. Stories shared around the dinner table with my grown sons differ from those I'd share with my grandmother or employer. Outfits I'd wear at a book signing or Comic Convention differ from what I'd wear to a funeral. I believe I'm demonstrating social intelligence by adapting my *surface* appropriately to any given situation.

We're all expected to "wear many hats" for the different situations in our lives, and now, in this age of global pandemic and social distancing—the very conditions that encouraged me to peek into the jigsaw-puzzling world—physical masks make it more challenging to look below the surface when we interact with others.

I'll gladly don a mask when I'm in pubic (well, to be honest, not *gladly*) to provide a pinch of protection for myself and others, but I'm truly glad I don't have to wear one at home. Still, there have been times when a mask at home might have been helpful in hiding my true feelings.

"You know, you don't have to finish it," my husband helpfully pointed out after suffering through my grumbling on more than one occasion. I suppose I'm not particularly good at presenting a poker-face mask when I'm frustrated. "It's a self-inflicted activity, right?"

Right. He's generally right. But you've probably figured out by now that I'm the kind of person who finds comfort in completing "self-inflicted" tasks—if they hold my attention—regardless of how important others may view those tasks.

Someone in a social media jigsaw group recently asked if she should complete a puzzle that bored her. She hated it. And although some of her puzzling peers encouraged her to push forward, to not let it defeat her, I and several others offered our dissenting opinions.

Life is too short for books, puzzles, movies, and people who bore you. There are too many great ones out there and certainly not enough hours in one lifetime to experience them all.

Mike and I give new movies the "15-minute rule," and I do the same with books. If they don't grab me in the first 15 minutes, turn it off. Give it away. Trash it if it's truly heinous—save others from suffering. And do it without compunction.

Yes, my 2,000-piece puzzle made me crazy and I often questioned my sanity while working on it. But it never bored me. I recalled past conversations with Nadine about establishing boundaries in different situations—mostly in terms of relationships—and decided I could apply her advice to my relationship with my puzzle. I would not allow it to consume *too* much of my time every day. Maybe just an hour in the morning right after coffee. Maybe two hours. Certainly no more than three hours if I'd had two cups of coffee.

Once I found those missing pieces, my relationship with the monster grew sweeter. I skimmed my fingers around the frame and over the mostly completed sections and marveled at how smooth and soft its surface felt. Tell me I'm not the only puzzler who does that, please. I've always appreciated pleasant tactile sensations, and this puzzle's surface was delightful.

You might be judging me right now. You may already have made a snap opinion about me from the photo in my bio. You might question why a woman my age strokes the surface of puzzles . . . and still collects marbles.

In the article *Snap-Judgment Science* by Nicholas Rule, he says, "Before we can finish blinking our eyes, we've already decided whether we want to hire, date, hate, or make friends with a person we're encountering for the first time."[41]

There's much written and many studies about this phenomenon, and I'll admit I've made my share of snap judgments. Even now I might decide instantaneously that someone is a jerk, a book is boring, and a puzzle is too easy, but I've learned that until I engage in a discussion, read a few pages, and pour the pieces onto a table, my initial impressions could be greatly skewed.

Yes, a "gut feeling" can often be accurate, but I'll remind myself to dig deeper, even if I end up following my gut. I'll remember surfaces can be deceiving. The surface of a lake may appear calm and flat as a mirror, but I know about the teaming life in its depths. The surface of our skin protects our gooey centers, but it can be pierced easily. The surface of the moon may look like blue cheese, but cows will continue to jump over it.

Have I digressed? And where *are* my cool, velvety smooth-surfaced marbles?

Speaking of marbles, my friend Hillery validated my 15-minute rule when she said some puzzles should be thrown away. Her comment shocked me. I never expected such a statement from a prolific puzzler. After she described a specific jigsaw puzzle with nothing but colorful marbles, I understood. At first glance, it was pretty. Then she discovered every piece was cut the same way, and every piece had the same four or five colors on it.

"It was just too painful," she said.

After spending some time in jigsaw puzzle social media groups, I've discovered there are those who live for puzzles like the one Hillery described, and those who abhor them—another reminder that we all matter, and we all see things from our own perspectives.

Marbles. Puzzles. Water. Skin. Expressions. Words. Covers. Masks.

Surfaces can be pretty, tough, soft, painful—come up with any adjective and apply it to the idea of a surface. Things may appear one way "on the surface," but when we look below, what we find can be startling, wonderful, frightening, enlightening . . . and in the case of a table surface, rewarding.

It's important to protect ourselves from deception and to look below the surfaces of people, ideas, and things in our lives before making major decisions. But that doesn't mean we should let what we discover stop us from tackling new challenges.

With the frame and three-quarters of my beautiful puzzle completed, all that remained was the stone wall and walkway to the front door. With a piece in my hand and peace in my heart, I focused on paving that walkway.

Nadine's Reflections

We make judgments so quickly, sometimes we don't even realize we have done it. Our brains are wired to efficiently assess a situation so we can respond in a timely manner. In many respects, this wiring is a positive attribute, especially in situations that could pose danger to us.

In some cases, however, our brain may pass judgment in error due to our distorted belief system, especially in regard to others. We tend to judge others harshly when we are insecure about ourselves, jealous, scared or intimidated, or when we lack understanding of differences. These judgments only cause hurt, perpetuate stereotypes, bring others down, and cause us to feel guilty.

We generally judge ourselves just as harshly. The best way to stop making such snap judgments is to educate ourselves in order to gain better understanding.

Try to look for the positive attributes in others and be more aware of your own negative thoughts. Avoid stereotyping and try to remember how it feels to be judged (we've all been on the receiving end). Focus on your own life and stop comparing yourself to others. This will lead to more personal contentment and positivity, which will enable you to become more open and accepting.

The next time you start to make a snap judgment/decision or "go with your gut," take a moment to make sure you have all the facts and a clear understanding of the person or situation.

With these thoughts in mind, reflect on the following questions:

- Are you guilty of making snap judgments? If so, what has been the result?

- Do you generally go with your "gut" feeling or do you do some research before making a decision?

- What stereotypes do you cling to?

- What expectations do you have for yourself? Are they realistic?

- Do you compare yourself to others? If so, what qualities do you generally envy in others?

- Does your comparison spur you to actions toward self-improvement or cause you to become depressed?

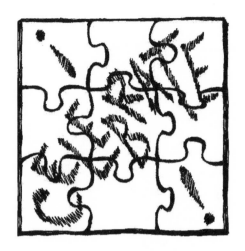

1O: CELEBRATE!

The last puzzle piece
Quietly clicks into place
Time to celebrate!

I didn't know about kissing the final piece until Nadine clued me in. I'm perfectly okay with establishing a healthy relationship with whatever puzzles I choose to engage in the future, but kissing that final piece?

I've done crazier things.

When Nadine is ready to place her final piece, she invites her husband to join her. After days of walking by her table with "Wows!" of amazement and encouragement as the pieces come together, John participates in the final thrill. Nadine hands him the piece, he places it in the final position, and together, they press the piece into place. Beautiful, right? And then, Nadine runs her fingers lightly over the surface! I was so happy when she told me she does this, because I thought I was the only weird one to do that.

When Mike walks by as I sit with a piece in hand and a perplexed expression on my face, he says "Wow" too, and occasionally follows it up with a comment about my sanity. I always laugh because he is well within his rights to point out my sometimes-compulsive pursuits.

"I promise not to turn this into a bowling thing," I told him somewhere around the placement of my 500th piece. See, back in the day, I joined a bowling league with a few other stay-at-home moms. We were horrible (I was the worst) and appropriately dubbed ourselves the "Gutter Girls." Well, when I started to improve and captured the attention of the alley manager, he groomed me for competition, and I ended up winning the Northern Virginia Bowler of the Year Award.

Mike didn't mind when I traded in the prize—a weekend trip for two to Las Vegas—for round-trip tickets to the island of Saint Croix. All those days of coming home smelling of Cheetos and beer paid off.

And I do have to remind myself that I have other obligations that don't revolve around "the puzzle table," as it will henceforth be called, but I'm meeting fascinating people and learning about more than just puzzling since I accepted the 2,000-piece challenge. I've barely explored the tip of the proverbial iceberg on which the world of jigsaw puzzlers sits.

I recently contacted Mark Lumb—administrator for the *Jigsaw Chill Zone* Facebook group and creator of the YouTube channel by the same name—about his puzzle completion ritual, and it's wonderful.

"I love doing the last 50 to 100 pieces of any puzzle as it is a family ritual for my two sons to take their places next to me and finish it together."

I suppose I should reevaluate the idea of working with others on my next puzzle. Evidently, it doesn't have to turn into a competition.

And Mark moves jigsaw puzzling to an entirely higher dimension by creating beautiful art from the puzzling process. After taking time-lapse photography at set intervals as a puzzle comes together, he then features the final product on his YouTube channel adding his own relaxing musical arrangements to the photos as one fades into the next until the composition is complete. His pieces are soothing, meditative . . . therapeutic, even.[42]

"I always take delight in recording the final piece that is placed by taking a photo of that event. It's very satisfying," he said.

I can relate to that feeling of satisfaction. When I was ready to set the 2,000[th] piece, like Mark does when he photographs his final placement, I had to document it.

I videoed walking to the table, picking up the piece, hoping it would fit into the final empty space—how could it not?—and clicking it into place. Victory! Those who saw my video thought it was a bit overly dramatic, but hey, the moment deserved drama. I've posted my exciting moment—"The 2,000[th] Piece"—on my YouTube channel along with other jigsaw videos.[43]

If you watch this video, however, you'll hear me say it will take another pandemic before I'll attempt another jigsaw puzzle. Completing this monster took a lot out of me, but surprisingly, it also filled me with excitement and opened my eyes to the world around me.

While I was creating my book *Haikus Can Amuse: 366 Haiku Starters*, I found myself thinking in the 5/7/5 rhythm of a haiku poem.[44] Likewise, by the time I committed to finishing the monster, I started framing everything around me as a puzzle scene.

While walking down our county road I'd notice the subtle differences in layers of gray obscuring the Sawatch Mountain Range as rain fell. How long would it take to sort all those tiny gray pieces? The little log cabin with the shiny red metal roof and cows in the field beyond would make a lovely pastoral scene. Swirling ripples atop Twin Lakes reflecting the surrounding snow-topped mountains as my paddleboard glides across its surface would make a particularly challenging puzzle. The work I did on my inaugural jigsaw made me infinitely more aware of the beauty and complexity of my surroundings.

So many gorgeous puzzles to be made.

As soon as I clicked in that last piece, I decided I probably wouldn't wait for the next global disaster to start a new puzzle. It's funny how once you've survived difficult challenges, the moments of anxiety, uncertainty, and back pain diminish in your memory.

That presentation I worked so hard to perfect is behind me and went better than I imagined. My suffering increased as I neared the summit of that 14,000' mountain, but I gasped at the views from the top, and not just because of the fall in atmospheric pressure. The excruciating pain of natural childbirth faded as soon as I held my child to my heart.

There are plenty of negatives in our world—always will be—and when something good happens or there is an accomplishment, the positive feelings we experience can be fleeting if we allow ourselves to go backward, to the past, to the misery. Let's not go there. Let's remind ourselves to focus on this moment. The past is no longer a thing we can control. Let it go.

When I focus on celebrating the good things in life and the positive aspects of myself and others, when I remember to be grateful, my outlook is always brighter and I feel wonderfully resilient. Even on days when I feel like crying, and do cry, I eventually refocus my attention on something beautiful or amusing—a blossom, a snowflake, a song, a duckling, a husband standing on his head, a completed puzzle—and I'm able to smile again.

I didn't have to wait long before starting my next puzzle. The pain of birthing my first huge jigsaw had barely worn off when I received a gift in the mail.

Nadine's daughter, Sarah—creator of this book's cover—sent photos of our last visit to a company and created a collage puzzle of highlights. Only 1,014 pieces! At first, I wasn't sure whether to laugh or cry. This was not a gift I could ignore. So I laughed and called to thank her for her thoughtfulness, and when I poured out the pieces onto the puzzle table, Mike walked by and said, "Wow."

Sarah had made copies for herself and for her mother too, so Mike agreed I had to complete what he called my "friendship puzzle." What a special gift.

You now may wonder why I would start my new career as a part-time puzzler with a 2,000-piecer. Was it because I figured every puzzle after that would be easier? Nope. One moment's glance into the online world of jigsaw puzzles and puzzlers taught me that future challenges could be intense: three-dimensional puzzles,

puzzles with no borders, puzzles with identical pieces, that marble puzzle I'd have to throw away, and wooden puzzles with "whimsy" pieces from a company my sister Susan Bernier Russo told me about called *Liberty Puzzles* in Boulder[45] (I just ordered my very first one).

The truth is, I'd purchased that particular monster puzzle the same day I purchased the silly 550-piece cow one before Nadine's first visit to our new home.[46] I knew nothing about how long any puzzle would take to complete, and we never got around to working on it. I remember saying something like, "We'll do this one next time you come," never imagining a pandemic would threaten our future plans.

And so, in the midst of a pandemic with no foreseeable end, I made the decision to construct the puzzle by myself. And then, with Nadine's professional guidance and contributions, we wrote the book she imagined. Instead of focusing on the bad news and fretting over things we couldn't control, we chose instead to work on creative endeavors and read words of enlightenment. Nadine referred me to author and Vipassana Meditation Teacher Jack Kornfield, who said, "Everything that has a beginning has an ending. Make your peace with that and all will be well."[47]

I worked on patience, and though I wasn't always successful, I persisted. I reminded myself I didn't have to eat the entire elephant in one sitting. I walked away and down the road when I felt overwhelmed, and then returned with renewed desire to appreciate how each tiny piece would contribute to the finished product. I cheered as I completed each little picture within the vast scene, and recognized that if I had asked for help, my experience could have been even more rewarding. I practiced different ways of focusing, remembered how a different perspective can enlighten, and when I got down on my knees to look below the surface of the puzzle table for my missing pieces, I stayed there for a moment and rejoiced.

Each of us will approach and respond to life's many challenges in unique ways. My Aunt Phyllis recently told me, "Just because it's hard, don't say 'I can't do it.'" She, along with others in her generation, faced challenges far greater than I have experienced in my lifetime, and I find inspiration in their resilience.

Even though it was a frivolous challenge when compared to many (if not most) other challenges in my life, completing my very first 2,000-piece jigsaw puzzle nevertheless refocused me on little daily lessons that continue to help me through difficult days.

I never consciously set out to "find peace" when I first dumped those colorful little bits onto my table, but somewhere along my journey with the pieces, that was exactly what I found.

What a bonus!

Nadine and I hope you may find comfort and validation in the pages of this book. We hope something in these pages helped you smile.

Piece by piece time heals
Many trials I've left behind
I find peace by piece

Nadine's Reflections

I love a good celebration. In fact, I would work hard to be the best, win, and get the prize. But what if you don't win? Is the hard work for nothing?

For many years, I was stuck in the trap of "all or nothing" thinking, a cognitive distortion that will most certainly drive you to push yourself hard and leave you feeling lousy if you don't win the prize. It wasn't until I learned to slow down, become more mindful, and enjoy the journey, that I was able to celebrate no matter the outcome. We can't all be winners all the time.

I've watched Laurel's husband, Mike, compete in 100-mile races over the last several years on mountain bike and on foot. His grit truly inspires me. In psychological terms, grit is defined as "a positive, non-cognitive trait based on an individual's perseverance of effort combined with the passion for a particular long-term goal or end state . . . This perseverance of effort promotes the overcoming of obstacles or challenges that lie on the path to accomplishment and serves as a driving force in achievement realization."[48]

Every year, with the exception of this year, hundreds of men and women gather in Leadville, Colorado to compete in a series of races in order to become a Leadman or Leadwoman. It is a grueling series and truly tests each participant's grit, as well as physical endurance. Of course, not everyone wins the title of Leadman or Leadwoman, but each person is celebrated, no matter the outcome.

It's all about the journey to the prize. Too many times we fail to recognize the journey, what we've learned, what we've accomplished along the way, and how we've grown as a person, a friend, an athlete, or a leader.

Since I am not much of an athlete, I revel in the completion of jigsaw puzzles. There have been a couple I have not fully completed, but I did not scold myself or feel bad. Instead, I celebrated what I did accomplish and what I learned about puzzling during the process. I've learned there are techniques for completing jigsaw puzzles. You can learn a lot on YouTube!

There are also other lessons I learned, or was reminded of, about life itself. Those lessons are the foundation of this book. They are also the foundation of my being, how I intend to live my life, and how I try to encourage others as a counselor.

I hope you have been inspired to reflect on your own life, to be open to change where needed, and to celebrate each step of your life's journey.

With these thoughts in mind, reflect on the following questions:

- Accomplishments deserve to be celebrated. How did you celebrate your latest accomplishment?

- Do you have any *rituals* you use in your celebrations?

- Over the course of a project, there are many ups and downs. Do you wait until you're finished to celebrate, or do you celebrate the small victories along the way?

- What value is there in acknowledging the journey as well as the goal?

- And finally, what do you do when you complete a new puzzle? Set it on fire? Store it away forever? Give it or throw it away? Redo it? Frame it? Place it under a glass-top table? Write a book about it? We would love to hear about your experiences!

AFTERWORD

From Laurel ~

As of this printing, the COVID-19 coronavirus pandemic lingers, and with no appreciable end in sight. People across the globe mourn the good old days of maskless social gatherings and never giving a second thought about going to the grocery store, to a doctor's appointment, or to church.

The world as we know it may never return to the normal we crave. But when I email my friend Nadine, I smile at her username: hope4321.

Despite the inconvenience of cumbersome new routines and the heartbreaking personal tragedies so many are enduring because of this pandemic, I remain hopeful for the future of our planet and its people. I believe in the myth of the Phoenix: Beautiful things will emerge from the chaos of our current times.

My collaboration with Nadine on this book—the first "group project" I've ever loved—reminds me of the positive, creative, and helpful spirits longing for expression in each of us. People worldwide are discovering new ways to move forward through the unknown. We are a resilient species. We will find a way to put this devastating foe into the history books that surely will be written about our triumph.

Some things must fall apart or be taken apart before they can be reconstructed, and my hope is for a more sensible "putting back together."

Disassembling my 550-piece cow puzzle with a visiting youngster and then having her older sisters stash away my 2,000-piece monster delighted me. I relegated the boxes to the past knowing the lessons I learned and remembered while tackling them will certainly make puzzling more enjoyable now and in the future.

I also reflected on another life lesson: Finding balance in work and in play. While Nadine and Sarah were here to finish up this book and cover design, we completed the challenging Liberty Puzzle I ordered as a celebratory treat. It took the three of us about eight hours to put it together. Remembering how Nadine invites her husband to join in the placement of the final piece, we cajoled mine into setting the last "whimsy" piece of the unique puzzle. And then? I whipped out a 100-piece glittery unicorn puzzle for Sarah and a 100-piece horse puzzle for Nadine!

Balance the tough with the fluff whenever possible.

I've also been humbled by what I thought was my tremendous accomplishment. As I continue to explore the world of jigsaw puzzling, I learn about people who have completed projects I might never consider attempting in my lifetime. And please, Sarah, *do not* buy me that 40,320-piece Ravensburger Disney Puzzle. Just . . . don't! I have ducks to feed, for goodness' sake!

Someday I *may* reassemble puzzles I've completed. I've already adopted Hillery's mother's practice of writing progress notes in the covers of those I now own. And someday the world and its inhabitants *will* emerge from under the ruinous consequences of this pandemic. I plan to witness this rebirth. I plan to sing the 1930s song "Happy Days are Here Again" at the top of my voice while doing a happy dance for the records.

In the meantime, I'll do my best to mindfully apply the lessons in this book to my daily life. I'll remember that although I'll never be perfect, I can always be better. I'll forever cherish the memories created during this joint endeavor with Nadine—which encompass far more than puzzling and writing—and along with a daily reminder to find something beautiful and something humorous in every day, I'll remain hopeful.

Time to start learning all the lyrics to that good-old-days song!

From Nadine ~

Just as the next puzzle brings joy and new challenges, so does each new day. I encourage you to take the lessons presented in this book and apply them to your life.

- Develop patience with yourself and others. Push back against life's challenges with persistence.
- Balance your time between work and leisure. Make time your friend, not your enemy.
- Set healthy boundaries that reflect your values and limits. Learn to say "no" and be loving, instead of "yes" out of obligation.
- Evaluate the strengths and qualities you bring to your relationships. Take an inventory of the quality of your relationships and the things that you value most. Don't be afraid to let the things that no longer bring you joy "fall away."
- Do "little things" each day that encourage others or enhance their lives. Remember that little things can have a big impact, like a raindrop causes ripples on a pond.

• Ask for help. You experience the love and care of others through their service, and they receive the joy that comes from doing something for another. It's a win-win. You may want to get assistance from a licensed counselor if there are areas of your life where you are facing overwhelming challenges. Help is readily available through online platforms as well as face-to-face.

• Remember to stay focused and live in the present moment. Don't allow thoughts of the past or future to steal time from your *Now*. Avoid depression and anxiety by practicing mindfulness.

• When you start to feel a negative emotion, take a moment to examine your thoughts and challenge them. Don't allow false perceptions and "stinking thinking" to cloud your judgment.

• Take every opportunity to strive to understand the reality of others before passing judgment. Low self-esteem, fear, jealousy, and lack of education can cause you to make snap judgments about others.

• Celebrate the journey, not just the accomplishment. You will experience increased motivation when you take time to acknowledge the completion of each step toward your goal.

I am grateful to have played a part in sharing these life lessons with you. I wish you love, joy, peace, happiness, and good health. Happy puzzling!

NOTES

1. Patience. (2020). Retrieved from
   https://dictionary.cambridge.org/us/dictionary/english/patience
2. Plautus, Titus Maccius. (n.d.). *Rudens, or The Fishermen's
   Rope*, act 2, scene 3. Retrieved from
   http://www.perseus.tufts.edu/hopper/text?doc=Perseus%3Atext
   %3A1999.02.0108%3Aact%3D2%3Ascene%3D3
3. Shakespeare, William. *Othello*, II, iii, 379.
4. Persist. (2020). Retrieved from
   https://dictionary.cambridge.org/us/dictionary/english/persist
5. For more on this Zen adage, go to:
   https://www.huffpost.com/entry/meditation_b_2382626
6. Lao Tzu, from the Tao Te Ching:
   http://thetaoteching.com/taoteching15.html
7. Tolstoy, Leo, *War and Peace* bk. X, ch. 16.
8. McHargue, L. (Host). (2020, April 18). *Episode 100: Q Diaires
   25* [Audio podcast]. Retrieved from
   https://soundcloud.com/laurelmchargue/episode-100-q-diaries-
   25
9. Tolle, Eckhart. *The Power of Now: A Guide to Spiritual
   Enlightenment.* Vancouver, B.C.: Namaste Publishing, Inc.,
   1997.
10. Mischel, Walter. *The Marshmallow Test: Why Self-Control is
    the Engine of Success*. Little, Brown & Company, 2015.
11. Mann, Thomas. *The Magic Mountain.* New York, NY: Alfred A.
    Knopf, Inc., 1995.
12. Templar, Richard. *The Rules of Life: A Personal Code for Living
    a Better, Happier, More Successful Life.* Upper Saddle River,
    NJ: Pearson Education Inc. publishing as FT Press, 2011, p. 84.
13. Wise Old Sayings. (2000-2020). Retrieved 10 June 2020, from
    https://www.wiseoldsayings.com/walking-away-quotes/
14. Campbell, Thomas. *Pleasures of Hope* [1799], pt. I, 1. 7 (from
    Bartlett's Familiar Quotations, John Bartlett, Fifteenth and 125th
    Anniversary Edition, p. 443).
15. Cloud, Henry, and John Townsend. *Boundaries: When to Say
    Yes, How to Say No to Take Control of Your Life.* Grand Rapids,
    MI: HarperCollins, 1992.
16. Benjamin Franklin Quotes. (1776). USHistory.org. Retrieved
    June 14, 2020, from USHistory.org Web site:
    https://www.ushistory.org/Valleyforge/history/franklin.html
17. Roedel, John. You can find more of Roedel's work on his
    Facebook page at: https://www.facebook.com/johnbigjohn, and
    in his books on Amazon.

18. For this sentence in the full poem "On Marriage" by Kahlil Gibran: https://www.poetryfoundation.org/poems/148576/on-marriage-5bff1692a81b0

19. Vincent Van Gogh Quotes. (1882). Website: Van Gogh Museum of Amsterdam: Vincent van Gogh Letters, Letter number: 274, Letter from: Vincent van Gogh, Location: The Hague, Letter to: Theo van Gogh, Date: October 22, 1882, Retrieved June 16, 2020, from Vangoghletters.org Web site: http://vangoghletters.org/vg/letters/let274/letter.html

20. Lao Tzu Quotes. (n.d.). Tao Te Ching, Ch. 63,Retrieved June 18, 2020 from wussu.com Web site: https://www.wussu.com/laotzu/laotzu63.html

21. Lamott, Anne. *Bird by Bird: Some Instructions on Writing and Life* New York, NY: Anchor Books, 1994, p. 19.

22. Quieros, Carlos j. (April 2009). *Sandra Cisneros: Facing Backwards, The 25th Anniversary of The House on Mango Street* [Article]. https://www.aarp.org/entertainment/books/info-04-2009/sandra_cisneros_house_on_mango_street_25th_anniversary.html

23. Hou, Kathleen. (September 2015). *Patti Smith on Being Strong, Happy, and Alive* [Article]. https://www.thecut.com/2015/09/patti-smith-on-being-strong-happy-and-alive.html

24. Chapman, Gary. *The Five Love Languages: The Secret to Love that Lasts*. Chicago, IL: Northfield Publishing, 2015.

25. Holiday, Ryan. *Ego is the Enemy*. New York, NY: Penguin Random House, 2016, p. 124.

26. Withers, B. (1972). Lean on Me [Lyrics]. Retrieved from https://www.lyrics.com/lyric/5044374/Lean+on+Me

27. Lennon, J. and McCartney, P. (1965). Help [Lyrics]. Retrieved from https://www.lyrics.com/lyric/9878520/The+Beatles/Help

28. According to http://www.cslewis.org/aboutus/faq/quotes-misattributed/, this quote is misattributed to C. S. Lewis, and should rather be attributed to "Rick Warren, *The Purpose Driven Life* OR *This Was Your Life! Preparing to Meet God Face to Face* by Rich Howard and Jamie Lash."

29. Buddha Quotes. (n.d.). BrainyQuote.com. Retrieved August 26, 2020, from BrainyQuote.com Web site: https://www.brainyquote.com/quotes/buddha_101052

30. Mindfulness. (2020). In *Oxford English Dictionary*. Retrieved from https://www.lexico.com/en/definition/mindfulness

31. Hanh, Thich Nhat. *The Miracle of Mindfulness: An Introduction to the Practice of Mindfulness*. Beacon Press, Boston, Massachusetts, 1975, p. 33.

32. Hanh, Thich Nhat. *The Miracle of Mindfulness: An Introduction to the Practice of Mindfulness.* Beacon Press, Boston, Massachusetts, 1975, p. 63.
33. Brach, Tara. *Radical Acceptance: Embracing Your Life with the Heart of a Buddha.* Bantam Dell, New York, New York, 2004, p. 44.
34. George Carlin Quotes. (n.d.). Goodreads.com. Retrieved August 26, 2020, from Goodreads.com Web site: https://www.goodreads.com/quotes/24059-some-people-see-the-glass-half-full-others-see-it
35. Nin, Anais. *Seduction of the Minotaur: The Authoritative Edition.* Sky Blue Press, 2010, Kindle edition, loc. 1981.
36. Shakespeare, William. *King Lear,* III, IV, 21.
37. Grohol, John M. (June 2019). *15 Common Cognitive Distortions* [Article]. https://psychcentral.com/lib/15-common-cognitive-distortions/
38. Burns, David D. *Feeling Good: The New Mood Therapy.* New York: New American Library, 2012.
39. Kahl, Oliver. [Cinegraf]. (2014, August 13). *O Captain, My Captain* [Video]. Youtube. https://youtu.be/j64SctPKmqk
40. Silverstein, Shel. *The Missing Piece.* New York, NY: HarperCollins Publishers, 1976.
41. Rule, Nicholas. (April 2014). *Snap-Judgment Science* [Article}. https://www.psychologicalscience.org/observer/snap-judgment-science
42. Lumb, Mark. [JigsawChillZone]. (n.d.). Home [YouTube Channel]. Retrieved from https://www.youtube.com/channel/UCkMD7sEIjonpjDZHMNWJcGw
43. McHargue, Laurel. [Laurel McHargue]. (n.d.). Home [YouTube Channel]. Retrieved from https://www.youtube.com/channel/UCZX5zYjl5tWHQkhb70gZJBw?view_as=subscriber
44. McHargue, Laurel. *Haikus Can Amuse: 366 Haiku Starters.* Leadville, CO: Alpha Peak LLC, 2016.
45. Liberty Puzzles website: https://www.libertypuzzles.com/about
46. The "monster" puzzle that inspired this book is a CEACO brand 2,000-piece puzzle titled "Coastal Escape," and the cow puzzle is the same brand, 550 pieces, titled "Selfies: Udderly Cool."
47. Kornfield, Jack. *Buddha's Little Instruction Book.* Bantam Books, New York, New York, 1994.
48. Grit. (2020). In Wikipedia. Retrieved from https://en.wikipedia.org/wiki/Grit_(personality_trait)

ABOUT THE AUTHORS

Laurel McHargue, a 1983 graduate of West Point, is the author of books in multiple genres, including the award-winning fantasy trilogy *Waterwight*, and the host of the podcast *Alligator Preserves*. A former Army Officer and public school teacher, she now lives and laughs and publishes and podcasts in Colorado's Rocky Mountains, where she also raises ducks.

Nadine Collier is a licensed professional counselor (LPC) and has been practicing for over twenty years. She lives in West Michigan with her husband, John, where they spend most of their summers boating and soaking in the sun on the beach. During the cold months, Nadine can be found reading, baking, and, of course, puzzling.

A Few More Words from Laurel

I would love to hear from you! Connect with me here:

Facebook: Leadville Laurel (author page)
Twitter: @LeadvilleLaurel
LinkedIn: Laurel (Bernier) McHargue
Web Page: www.laurelmchargue.com
Email: laurel@strackpress.com
Podcast: Alligator Preserves

Check out my other books on my **Amazon Author page**
and let me know what you think!

And remember, we struggling
authors/musicians/artists/actors love positive feedback,
so if you like what we do, please consider writing
reviews of our work! If you don't like what we do, well,
if you can't say something nice . . .

Sarah Collier (with unknown llama behind her),
Laurel McHargue, and Nadine Collier: The Friendship puzzle!

Also by Laurel McHargue:

Waterwight: Book I of the Waterwight Series: In a post-cataclysmic world threatened by stinking ooze, a brave girl searches for her missing parents with the help of talking animals and evolving powers...while a malicious shapeshifter tries to stop her!

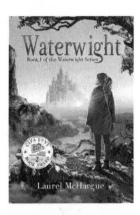

Waterwight Flux: Book II: Has Celeste cured the chaos in her shattered world? Nick and the villagers must defend themselves without her, and jealous ancient gods have selfish ideas about how they'll use the girl who stopped the ooze!

Waterwight Breathe: Book III: Celeste regains consciousness with powerful new abilities. The gods are in trouble, and Celeste must decide how, or if, she will help them. With insane scientists plotting to subjugate her village, she and her friends rally for a final confrontation!

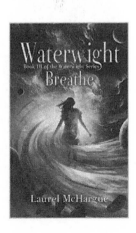

Haikus Can Amuse!:
Perfect homeschooling tool! Discover the creativity this haiku book will unleash in you! Explore your emotional responses as you complete unique poems with 366 first-line prompts and topics provided for you.

"Miss?": Maggie, a feisty young Army veteran, believes her new life as a 7th grade English teacher will be a breeze, but quickly finds out how wrong she is. Despite daily challenges, however, she finds ways to reach her struggling students, and must ultimately make a painful decision.

Hai CLASS ku: A fun homeschooling tool! A full semester's worth of daily Language Arts activities! Discover the creativity this haiku book will unleash in students! Ninety first-line prompts and topics provided to stimulate the imagination, with space to draw and journal.